PROJECT SOLOMON

The True Story of
a Lonely Horse
Who Found a Home—
and Became a Hero

TYNDALE
MOMENTUM®

A Tyndale nonfiction imprint

Jodi Stuber &
Jennifer Marshall Bleakley

Visit Tyndale online at tyndale.com.

Visit Tyndale Momentum online at tyndalemomentum.com.

Tyndale, Tyndale's quill logo, *Tyndale Momentum*, and the Tyndale Momentum logo are registered trademarks of Tyndale House Ministries. Tyndale Momentum is a nonfiction imprint of Tyndale House Publishers, Carol Stream, Illinois.

Project Solomon: The True Story of a Lonely Horse Who Found a Home—and Became a Hero

Designed by Julie Chen

Edited by Bonne Steffen

Published in association with Jessica Kirkland and the literary agency at Kirkland Media Management, LLC.

For information about special discounts for bulk purchases, please contact Tyndale House Publishers at csresponse@tyndale.com, or call 1-855-277-9400.

Library of Congress Cataloging-in-Publication Data

A catalog record for this book is available from the Library of Congress.

ISBN 978-1-4964-6309-8 (HC)
ISBN 978-1-4964-5531-4 (SC)

Printed in the United States of America

28   27   26   25   24   23   22
7   6   5   4   3   2   1

To the loves of my life: Ty, Jessica, Richard, and Hope

JODI STUBER

For Darrell, Andrew, and Ella

JENNIFER MARSHALL BLEAKLEY

Before You Begin

ALL THE EVENTS IN THIS BOOK are drawn from real life. In order to protect the privacy of the children and veterans who are part of the HopeWell community, certain characters' names and details have been changed, and a few are composites of different individuals' experiences. Some events and timelines have been compressed for brevity and to tell a more cohesive story.

As I write this, several of the animals mentioned in the book still reside at HopeWell, where they continue to play an active role in HopeWell's mission of creating an environment where children and adults—including veterans, current military service men and women, and their families—can experience love, hope, redemption, and the power of finding purpose, even in the midst of pain.

Jennifer Marshall Bleakley

Prologue

Jodi's forearms ached as she pounded the posthole digger into the ground. Chunks of soil gave way as she repeatedly twisted the metal blades against the hardened earth. Satisfied with the depth, she heaved a wooden post into place. *Did that make six or seven?* She had lost count. Using her foot, she pushed the mound of dirt back in the hole.

Empty.

Refill.

Empty.

Refill.

If only the human spirit could be refilled as easily as a hole in the ground.

She tamped the soil around the post until it felt secure. Satisfied with her work, Jodi counted off another ten feet and started the process again. Her hands began to cramp. But she wouldn't stop. She couldn't. The physical pain throbbing in her arms offered a welcome, albeit temporary, reprieve from the searing pain in her heart.

Jodi thrust the heavy digger against the ground. Small rocks and dried grass went flying. She pushed a strand of blonde hair out of her face, leaving a streak of dirt behind. Stopping for a moment, she pulled off her gloves, gathered her hair, and forced the wayward wisps back into a ponytail. She cast a glance at the line of posts dotting the untamed landscape.

Had it only been three years since they bought the land?

It felt like a lifetime.

Once a thriving farm, the unused land had been overrun with vegetation. Tall grass now swayed in the slight breeze. Vines hung like curtains over abandoned machinery. And large logs lay scattered across the acreage—the rotting wood providing refuge and nourishment to colonies of insects.

Returning to her work, she jammed the metal blade in the hole and hit a large rock. The jolt of pain that radiated up her arm brought everything to a halt.

What am I doing? It's Memorial Day weekend! I should be barbecuing with Ty and the kids.

The fence had seemed like a good idea in the middle of the night. Actually, it had felt less like an idea and more like a command. Maybe even a calling?

The noonday sun seemed even hotter than usual, as she began to question her memory of the night before—as well as her sanity.

Maybe I really am losing it. They say grief can do that to a person.

Moving past her moment of doubt, Jodi kept going. She kept digging and planting fence posts and refilling holes and tamping the earth.

Even though they didn't need a fence.

She had no horses. No cattle. Not even a garden.

But something was driving her forward. A yearning like she had never known kept her arms moving, even as her muscles protested. A promise—whispered to her hurting soul in the middle of the night—kept her mind focused on one thing, and one thing alone: *Build a fence.*

This yearning—this calling—felt bigger than her grief.

Bigger than a dream.

As the sun began its descent toward the treetops, Jodi finally leaned on the posthole digger and looked at what she had accomplished.

Wooden posts stood in formation—guardians of an overgrown field.

Jodi arched her back. Every muscle ached, but her muscles had nothing to do with the sudden quiver radiating through her heart.

"I can see it," she whispered in elated disbelief. Tears made muddy streaks down her cheeks. "I can see it . . ."

1

FOUR YEARS LATER

JODI REACHED ACROSS THE PASSENGER SEAT of her van, fumbling for the scrap of paper with the directions she had written down. "There you are!" She held the paper against the steering wheel and tried to decipher her scribbles. She had been so distracted the day Ken called that she had hurriedly jotted down the basic information before rushing back to her four-page to-do list. Now she wished she had spent a few extra seconds writing legibly.

The afternoon sun in her eyes made it difficult to read the street signs. She drove past one, then slowed down at the next.

"I think this is the right road," she mumbled, turning off the two-lane highway onto a dirt road.

She glanced again at the last line of directions: *Last house. Past open field. Dead end.*

A Road Ends sign a few feet ahead boosted her confidence as she continued down the narrow road, made even narrower by the closely placed trees and thick underbrush. There was barely enough room for her vehicle to pass.

She glanced out at a white farmhouse, almost hidden behind a curtain of evergreens. A gust of wind snatched and swirled some leaves in front of her like tiny colorful kites freed from their strings. The orange, red, and yellow leaves swooped and fluttered in the wind. Clouds were billowing to the north.

I'm glad I grabbed a coat before I left. Since she had lived in Michigan her entire life, she knew the unseasonably warm temperatures they were experiencing in mid-October would not last much longer. The wind and gathering clouds hinted at colder weather.

Jodi came upon a field overrun with at least a dozen giant rolls of hay. *That must be the field.* She stopped the van for a moment.

"And that's *a lot* of hay," she marveled out loud, gratitude warming her heart. "That will last quite a while."

With eight horses, one donkey, and four goats needing to be fed twice a day, she was in constant need of hay and money to buy it. Then it hit her. *How are we going to get all this back to the ranch?*

"I'll let Ty figure that one out," she chuckled, grateful for a husband who enjoyed a good challenge and didn't shy away from hard work.

Jodi eased off the brake as a driveway came into view at the bottom of a gentle slope. She followed the driveway to a tan ranch-style house surrounded by rolling hills and open fields.

As she pulled in behind a large pickup truck, she inhaled deeply, held it for a few seconds, and then slowly exhaled.

It was time to see what was in store for the hay donation. Jodi's heart beat faster. *What if it doesn't work out? What if I can't agree to their conditions? What if it turns out badly?*

What-ifs had plagued Jodi her whole life . . . a default setting she had fought hard to reset.

"And what if it works out just fine, Jodi Stuber?" she said aloud, refusing to allow her fear to get the upper hand. "Stop letting fear lead."

Her pep talk worked—at least for the moment—and her fear began to give way to a hopeful anticipation. It was the same hopeful anticipation she had experienced the week before during the Cowboy Ball—the annual fall fundraiser supporting HopeWell, their therapy ranch. She and Ty had founded the ranch three years ago, a year after Jodi had set up the fence posts. Those four years had flown by, and Jodi knew that not only the clients had benefited from the therapy, but she had too. Still, running the ranch required a lot of funds, and fundraising was Jodi's least favorite part of her job. Yet it was vital to care for the menagerie of animals—horses, donkeys, goats, chickens, ducks, rabbits, and dogs.

Each year, the Cowboy Ball was a lot of fun to put on, but Jodi and her small team of volunteers spent months planning, weeks gathering and packaging donations to auction off, and days decorating the venue to make it happen. This year's was no exception. By the time the actual event rolled around, she was mentally and physically exhausted.

That day, with just two hours left before the guests would arrive, Jodi had run home from the ranch to shower and change.

Then she had allowed herself ten quiet minutes before heading to the banquet hall. Two minutes into her short respite, her phone rang. Jodi didn't recognize the number and didn't have the energy to answer, so she let the call go to voice mail. "Eight more minutes," she breathed out, sinking into the closest chair.

So much was riding on this event. The fundraiser would make or break their budget for the year. "Please, God, let us meet our goal," she prayed. Her phone chimed a voice mail alert. *What if it's the caterer? Or someone is calling about an emergency? What if there is a water main break or a gas leak in the building? Oh, why didn't I answer!* Jodi lamented, quickly playing back the voice mail.

"Hi, Jodi, my name is Ken Brigham. We have a mutual friend who gave me your number. He's been telling my wife, Sue, and me about the good work you all are doing."

All is well at the venue. Jodi's breathing slowed as she listened to the rest of Ken's message.

"Just now on the radio we heard about the fundraiser you're hosting, and Sue and I decided to call to make a donation. And a pretty large one at that. If you'll give me a call back, we'd love to discuss it with you."

Jodi's head spun from the emotional whiplash she had just given herself. A large donation!

"Wow, God, you sure work fast." She laughed, hitting the call back on her phone.

Depending on the amount Ken wanted to give, they might meet their financial goal for the night—even before the event began! Maybe they would far exceed their goal this year. Jodi's cheeks flushed with the thought.

Of course, sometimes people wanted to donate farm

equipment or building supplies, which would certainly qualify as a large donation—at least in size. *Is that what he meant?* Jodi fought to keep her voice steady and gracious when Ken answered the phone.

"Well, that was a quick call back," he said, laughing.

Jodi suddenly wished she had played it a little cooler and called him back the next day, but it was too late now. Might as well own her eagerness.

"You certainly know how to get someone to return your call," she joked. "I'm actually on my way to our Cowboy Ball fundraiser now, but I wanted to get back to you before the evening got away from me. Ken, thank you so much for thinking of donating to HopeWell."

"Oh, you betcha," Ken replied. "We've been hearing how you and your horses are helping so many in our community, and we feel like—" there was a slight hesitation before he continued— "well, we feel like we have something that should really belong to you."

Jodi was curious, but also slightly disappointed. She got the distinct feeling Ken was not talking about money. Her dream of being fully funded before the event officially began started to fade. But she quickly shook off the feeling, reminding herself that anyone willing to give anything to HopeWell deserved her gratitude, respect, and attention.

"Well, I am most intrigued," she said, standing to stretch her back.

"We have a lot of hay that we would like for you to have. A dozen large rolls actually. And as an extra bonus—or I guess maybe it's more like a condition," he clarified with a short chuckle, "the hay comes with a horse! A six-year-old gelding named Harley."

Jodi sank back into her chair. *A horse?* she mouthed.

"Harley is such a good boy and has brought our family nothing but love and joy. And he's a natural with kids. But we just aren't able to give him what he needs anymore. We believe you can. And, well, we'd really like you to meet him and hear our story. And if you agree with us, we'd like him to go to HopeWell."

Jodi walked to the kitchen sink and looked out the window toward the horses grazing in the field. She hadn't planned on adding another horse to their herd. Eight really did seem like enough. In fact, when it came to the budget, eight often felt like too many. But something in Ken's voice made her consider his offer. And the man certainly deserved to have someone hear his story. Jodi couldn't offer people much, but she could listen to what they wanted to share. And, yes, HopeWell could certainly use the hay.

Jodi took a deep breath before responding.

"Ken, I would be honored to come out and meet Harley. And we would be so grateful for the generous offer of hay. Would next week be okay?"

After deciding on a day and time, Jodi scribbled his address and directions on some junk mail lying on the counter. When she hung up, she tore off the piece with the needed information and tucked it in her day planner. It was time to head to the fundraiser.

Jodi wasn't too worried. She knew from past experiences that her adrenaline would surge the moment the first guest arrived. And it did. Dinner was delicious, her talk was well received, and the live auction was as entertaining as it was profitable. They certainly didn't raise a huge surplus of funds, but they raised enough to meet HopeWell's day-to-day needs for the next year.

Now, as Jodi sat parked outside of Ken and Sue's house, she shook off all thoughts of last week and pulled the key from the ignition. It was time to focus on the task at hand. Yet, she couldn't help but wonder if they had raised enough money during the fundraiser to add another horse to the herd. The hay she had passed driving in would go a long way toward feeding the herd, but another horse would mean increased veterinarian and farrier bills, as well as extra time training a new horse to work with the kids and adults they served.

Jodi tucked her sunglasses and the scrap of paper safely into the side pocket of her purse and grabbed some pamphlets about HopeWell from the glove box. As she got out of the van, something to the right of the house caught her attention. A deer—a small doe—was standing perfectly still, her head raised, her gaze fixed on something off in the distance. Jodi was surprised to find a deer standing so close to a house in the middle of the day.

"What are you doing out here, little one?" she asked taking a few tentative steps toward the doe. "Are you okay?"

Suddenly, a twig snapped under Jodi's foot. She jumped, but the doe didn't move—not even a twitch. Jodi squinted against the late afternoon sun . . . then laughed out loud.

"You're not real, are you?" she said, chuckling and shaking her head. "Leave it to me to be concerned over a plastic deer!"

Jodi walked up three steps to the porch, but before she could knock, the door opened.

"Well, you must be Jodi."

"And you must be Ken and Sue," she replied, nodding her head at the woman standing just behind Ken.

"Guilty as charged," the couple said, welcoming her inside.

Ken and Sue appeared to be in their mid- to late-forties—not much older than she and Ty. Sue led the way to the dining room where she had set out tea and fresh baked cookies. The three of them engaged in easy conversation—discussing the impending cold front and lamenting the end of the mild temperatures. As they finished their tea, the conversation turned to horses.

Horses were one of Jodi's favorite subjects and had been since the age of five when she begged her parents for a white pony. She promised to keep the pony in her bedroom and feed it hamburgers and cookies. Thirty-five years later, she had gotten her pony, and several horses too. Thankfully in that time, she had learned that horses fare much better in open, outdoor spaces and get more nourishment from hay and grain.

"So tell me a little about Harley," Jodi said, sensing the couple's eagerness to share their story with her.

Ken and Sue's faces lit up. Their affection for Harley was obvious. Then she remembered what Ken had said to her on the phone. "You can give Harley something we can't." *What could that be?*

"Our boy is lonely," Sue began, answering Jodi's unspoken question. "For years we had three horses, our three musketeers. They were the best of friends. Even though health problems prevented Ken and me from doing much riding, the horses brought us a lot of happiness. We loved watching them in the field and taking care of them. But two years ago, we lost our oldest gelding; then last year we lost our mare. Harley was left all by himself, and the poor boy is terribly lonesome."

Lonesome. Jodi's throat tightened when Sue said the word. A familiar emptiness settled around her like a well-worn shawl.

"I am so very sorry for your loss."

Sue nodded. "Thank you. It's been hard for us and Harley."

"A couple of months ago I came home from work to find Harley standing just as content as could be beside that plastic deer in the front yard," Ken said. "He had broken out of the pasture. I guess he figured a plastic friend was better than no friend at all."

Jodi didn't know whether to laugh or cry. The image of a large horse standing beside a small plastic deer was as funny as it was heartbreaking.

"After Harley broke out the fourth time, we knew he deserved better." Ken took his wife's hand. "But we just can't afford to take on more horses."

"I was talking to a friend about our situation, and she mentioned your farm," Sue explained. "She said you are helping families cope with some heavy issues by letting them work with your horses. We think Harley would be a good fit for your ranch. And I just love the name—HopeWell. It just feels right, you know?"

"I know exactly what you mean," Jodi said. The ranch had become a well of hope for her and so many others. "Is it okay for me to meet Harley?"

Ken's jovial expression returned as he stood.

The three of them walked behind the house where a beautiful chestnut quarter horse was standing in the middle of a field.

"Come on over here, Harley boy," Ken called out.

Harley's head popped up, and his ears flicked up in attention. He walked directly to Ken at the fence line and greeted him. Ken leaned his head against Harley's muzzle. The scene felt so private that Jodi momentarily looked away. Then Harley started frisking Sue for treats. His fuzzy gray lips rooted around the woman's shoulders, then he stretched his head over the fence and began inspecting her pockets.

"Okay, okay," Sue laughed. "I surrender." She pulled a treat out of her back pocket and offered it to Harley, who eagerly accepted her offering.

Jodi stood several feet away from the fence to observe Harley interacting with his owners. Ty would be arriving soon with Ryan, their farrier and horse trainer, and Aimee, a HopeWell volunteer and veterinarian student. Jodi had asked the three of them to help assess the horse. Something deep inside of Jodi told her that Harley would be joining their herd, but she needed to consult the team.

Ken cleared his throat.

"I've always felt Harley was a special boy," he said, absently stroking his horse. "But a few months ago, I discovered just how special he is."

"What happened?"

"Our daughter brought the kids over for a visit. After lunch the kids went outside to play hide-and-seek. Colin, our five-year-old grandson, decided he was going to find a good hiding spot. He definitely did. After a while, his brother asked us to help find Colin. Sue suggested I check the barn and Harley's run-in shelter, but I couldn't imagine the boy would have gone out there. He's such a little thing, you know?"

Jodi could see Ken was reliving the moment.

"While the rest of the family spread out around the yard, I went to the barn. The door was shut tight, and it was pretty dark in there. I called Colin's name, but he didn't answer. So I went to Harley's run-in shelter. Harley was inside resting, but as I got closer, I noticed something else—something that stopped me in my tracks. Colin was sitting without a care in the world under Harley!"

Jodi couldn't imagine finding a child sitting underneath a thousand-pound horse. Even though her own children were teenagers, she still drilled a fearful respect of horses into them.

"What did you do?" she asked, her words just above a whisper.

Ken chuckled. "I fought every instinct I had to shout out for the boy. I casually walked up to Harley and quietly asked Colin what he was doing.

"'I'm hiding, Grandpa,' he said. I told him that Harley is not a hiding spot; he is a big horse with heavy feet, and he might accidentally step on him."

"What did Colin do?" Jodi asked.

"He looked at Harley, then at me, and said, 'No, he won't, Grandpa. Harley is careful.'"

Jodi couldn't help but laugh.

"Well, good ol' Harley never moved. Not an inch. Not a muscle. He just stood as still as can be. Not the least bit bothered by the visitor beneath his belly." Ken rubbed Harley's chin.

"So how did you get Colin to move?"

"I did the only reasonable thing a man could do in that situation. I bribed my grandson with ice cream. Worked like a charm too."

"That would have worked for me too."

Jodi studied Harley's current stance and expression. One back hoof was cocked, his lips were relaxed, and his ears were turned to the sides. He was the picture of a contented, peaceful horse. *A gentle giant.*

Ken and Sue described other instances of Harley with their grandchildren. "He has never reacted with anything other than patience and gentleness," Ken said.

"Are you sure you don't want to keep Harley for them?" Jodi asked.

"No, he's just so lonely for a herd," Sue explained. "And our grandkids aren't able to visit us that often. We would love to keep Harley, but we want him to have a good life."

Ken nodded in agreement.

Jodi heard car doors close in the distance. Her team must have arrived. Ken put his hand up.

"Sue and I can meet your team and bring them over here. Why don't you get to know Harley for a bit?"

"I think that sounds like a wonderful idea."

As the couple walked away, Jodi approached Harley. She stopped a foot from the fence. Harley flicked an ear in her direction as he pulled at a clump of grass. Jodi kept her hands at her sides and her posture relaxed. She wanted to make it clear to Harley that she was not a threat.

"Hello, Harley," she said softly. "I'm Jodi."

Harley raised his head, his dark eyes focused on Jodi.

"I sure am glad to meet you," she whispered.

Harley took three steps forward, his lips moving as if chewing an invisible wad of gum. He and Jodi observed each other across the fence. Jodi longed to reach her hand out and run it down the length of the thin white stripe on his muzzle. But she wouldn't rush him. She would let Harley make the first move.

"I hear you've been a bit lonely out here. Your deer friend isn't such great company, huh?" Jodi kept her voice upbeat and soft. Harley's ears flicked in response to her words. "It's hard to be lonely isn't it, Harley? It's hard to miss someone who should be here."

Jodi's words trailed off. She closed her eyes and took a deep breath. *Focus, Jodi,* she commanded herself. *Be present.*

A loud equine exhale startled her from her thoughts.

Harley's face was inches from hers. The coarse hair from his chin tickled her cheek. A moment later, the large horse rested his chin on Jodi's shoulder and exhaled again. She turned her face and breathed out in return—greeting him as another horse would. Jodi slowly reached up and gently rested her right hand on Harley's neck. She could see her reflection in Harley's left eye. "Sweet one, you are not going to be lonely anymore."

The two stood together, inhaling and exhaling.

"Well, it appears our presence here might be a bit irrelevant," Jodi heard Ty say. "I can't leave you alone for a second without a handsome stud finding you!"

"He's a gelding," Jodi corrected, trying not to disturb Harley.

"You can admit it. You have a weakness for the tall, dark, and handsome type—as long as they have four legs and a tail, that is," Ty said, with a laugh.

"Well, guys," she said, turning her attention to the human herd, "it looks like it's time to introduce you to the newest addition to HopeWell. I mean, of course, if you all agree," she amended, sheepishly.

"Let's check this boy out," Ryan said, climbing though the fence rails.

Jodi and Aimee jokingly rolled their eyes as they entered

through the gate. Ken retrieved Harley's tack from the nearby barn. The horse stood perfectly still as Ryan saddled him and mounted. It was clear that Harley had no problem with a rider. Ryan asked Harley to back up, to go forward, and to walk. The horse responded to each request. As Ryan put Harley through his paces, Aimee observed his gait and temperament. Then Ryan dismounted and took off Harley's saddle so Aimee could examine the horse's skin, hooves, and teeth. When she was done, she gave Jodi a thumbs-up.

"He looks to be a healthy, compliant gelding," Aimee declared.

Ken and Sue beamed like proud parents. Yet behind their smiles Jodi could sense an ache. She imagined it would feel a lot like finding out your child had been accepted to a faraway college. It was the beginning of an exciting new chapter of life, but also the end of a chapter you have loved. Jodi's heart swelled with gratitude and appreciation, and she made a mental note to send them periodic updates about Harley.

Harley.

It was such a good name, and yet Jodi liked to give each of the HopeWell horses a new name as they embarked on a new life.

While Ryan and Aimee put the tack away, and Ty made arrangements with Ken and Sue for transporting the horse, Jodi stood quietly with Harley. He lowered his head and ripped several tall blades of grass from the ground, with one blade clinging to his bottom lip. His eyes flitted to hers.

"You have very wise eyes," she whispered.

The horse took two steps toward Jodi.

"And the way you instinctively knew what to do when little

Colin hid under your belly shows that you have a very wise mind too."

The horse closed the distance between them.

"What do you think about the name Solomon? He was the wisest man who ever lived. He was also a king. Regal like you."

The horse pressed his muzzle to Jodi's face and breathed out.

"I'll take that as a yes."

Jodi looked up. Everyone was staring at her and Harley with hopeful expressions. The stakes suddenly felt incredibly high. The what-ifs she had kept at bay for the past two hours started rapid-firing in her mind.

2

"Do you think he's okay back there?" Jodi asked Ty. She twisted around in her seat as far as the seatbelt would allow. "I can't see him through that tiny little window in the front of the trailer."

They had waited three weeks to get the results of the Coggins blood test Solomon underwent—a test required by Michigan to check for the presence of equine infectious anemia, a highly contagious and potentially fatal disease. The test results had been negative, which meant no quarantine, so Jodi was eager to get Solomon to his new home.

Jodi called Tania—the volunteer coordinator and official kid-wrangler at HopeWell—to let her know they were fifteen minutes from the ranch.

"We're ready for you," Tania said. "Solomon will have quite the welcome committee."

Jodi always loved bringing a new horse to the ranch. Since the day she and Ty first opened HopeWell, they had celebrated well over a dozen new arrivals, and the excitement never ceased to delight her.

"Do you remember the day we brought Promise to HopeWell?" Jodi asked Ty after hanging up with Tania.

"How could I ever forget our first horse—the exact breed of horse you had wanted as a child?" Ty said. "That was actually my first clue that HopeWell was going to be more than just a ranch. And as if that wasn't enough, the very next day we found out about two more horses in need of a home—two more of your favorite breeds you had wished for as a kid."

It was true. When Jodi was five years old, she had begged her parents for a white pony; when she was twelve, she wanted a thoroughbred like the first horse she had ridden; when she was sixteen, her heart was set on a sorrel quarter horse with white socks, like the one she had worked with in the 4-H program. Each of the horses from her past had pointed her to a God she had not yet known, helped heal hurts she hadn't been able to verbalize, and planted seeds of hope within her heart. As a kid, she never could have imagined that those special horses would one day help lead her to start a therapy ranch.

"I still can't believe God brought us those specific horses."

As Ty turned the pickup onto one of the gravel roads that led to HopeWell, Jodi glanced back to make sure the trailer was still attached.

"I haven't lost one yet," her husband said with a chuckle.

A few minutes later, the packed dirt drive to the ranch came into view. The moment Jodi saw the "Welcome to HopeWell" sign made from old horseshoes, she relaxed.

Home.

As they passed the outdoor arena and round pen on the right, Jodi couldn't help but whisper a prayer of thanks for how far they had come. Granted, there was still a long way to go. They desperately needed to finish assembling the covered arena they had been able to purchase at a deep discount from a local man named Kurtis, a kind-hearted veteran who supported HopeWell's mission. An indoor arena would allow them to offer sessions in inclement weather, but they still had a lot of work to do before it was functional. It would also be nice if Jodi could pay herself a small salary someday—and maybe even hire a few staff. But they were managing. And more important to Jodi, people were finding peace and experiencing healing for deep hurts.

Yes, having more would be nice, but she couldn't be anything but grateful for what they did have. As Ty pulled into the parking area near the HopeWell office, she saw them. More than twenty children were standing in front of the large pasture holding signs and banners welcoming Solomon to his new home. And behind them were several adults, looking just as excited. The entourage was complete with the HopeWell herd, all standing at the fence, lined up as if arranged for a photo shoot. Jodi could barely keep from crying.

"They do that every time, don't they?" Ty asked, looking in the horses' direction.

"They do!" Jodi said enthusiastically. "I think they are as curious and excited as the rest of us—probably more so—to find out who's inside this trailer."

A sudden wave of stress rippled through Jodi at the thought of what the next few days would bring. Integrating a new horse into an established herd was challenging. And as much as she loved bringing a new horse to the ranch, she dreaded the process of introducing him or her to the herd. In an equine herd, hierarchy is everything, and rankings are often challenged and re-established, with a constant jockeying of position. All of which means the newest horse usually becomes the bottom-most horse. And the established herd makes sure he or she knows it. From kicking to shunning, to chasing and nipping, the new horse is given a clear message. Granted, things tend to calm down as the horses become accustomed to each other, but those first few days can be quite stressful for everyone—equine and human alike.

As Ty parked the truck and turned off the engine, Jodi spotted their sixteen-year-old daughter, Jessica, and fifteen-year-old son, Richard. Both were leaning on the porch railing of the modular home used for the HopeWell office. *They're here!* Jodi's entire face lit up. She waved enthusiastically. Jessica returned the gesture with a brief raise of her hand, while Richard dipped his head in a quick nod. Jodi didn't mind their lack of enthusiasm one bit. She was just delighted the teenagers had decided to participate.

The couple climbed out of the truck and were immediately surrounded by children.

"What's he look like, Ms. Jodi?"

"How big is he?"

"Can I ride him?"

Jodi smiled at the children, trying to make eye contact with each one, before addressing them as a group.

"Thank you, all, for being here! Solomon is a sweet boy with a reddish-brown coat, black eyes, and a little white line down his face. He is big, but not too big. And I'm sure after he gets used to his new home, he will love meeting all of you. But first we need to get him unloaded and then let him get settled."

The children jumped up and down. All except one little girl, who tugged on the bottom of Jodi's coat. Her name was Shontell.

"What is it, honey?" Jodi asked, bending over to look the girl in the eyes.

"Was Solomon sad to leave his family?"

Jodi put her hand on the child's shoulder. Jodi knew that Shontell had been in the foster care system for more than half her young life, so her concern for Solomon didn't surprise Jodi at all.

"Shontell, thank you for asking that. I'm so glad Solomon is going to have such a kind and understanding friend here. You know what? I am sure Solomon is going to miss his human family. They loved him very much. But he was very lonely there. His horse friends had died, and he was all by himself most of the time. I imagine he will feel sad for a while, but I think he will eventually feel happy to have lots of new friends and a big new family to love and take care of him. What do you think?"

Shontell squinted as she tried to glimpse the horse in the trailer. "I think he will be happy here too."

God, thank you for this sweet girl. Please protect her precious heart, Jodi prayed silently.

"Well, are we going to stand around this trailer all day, or are we going to unload a horse?" Ty asked the crowd.

"Unload the horse!"

Tania led the children to the pavilion where they would have a clear view without being in any danger. A few adult volunteers went to open the gate to the small field where Solomon would spend his first few days. It was adjacent to the large field where most of the herd was kept. The arrangement allowed the horses to greet each other and get used to each other while maintaining a clear boundary between them.

Jodi entered the side door at the front of the trailer. "Hey, buddy," she spoke softly. "How are you doing?"

Solomon was on high alert, watching Jodi's every move.

"Ready to meet your new family?" she asked, untying his lead rope from the hook.

Solomon stomped the trailer floor as Ty unlatched the large rear door. Solomon needed no other instruction or invitation. He immediately began backing up as if he had done it every day of his life. Loading him had taken them a good forty-five minutes, but this was going to be quick. As Jodi held his lead rope and followed him out, squeals of delight and a rush of voices floated from the pavilion.

"There he is!"

"I see him!"

"Move! I wanna see him too!"

Solomon froze the moment all four hooves were on the ground. His ears moved around like radar dishes searching for the source of each new sound.

"You're fine, boy," Jodi soothed. "You just have some adoring fans who are excited to meet you."

Several whinnies joined the young voices. Solomon's ears flicked at the new sounds.

Jodi leaned toward the horse. "Your welcome committee seems to be growing by the minute. Be patient with your new herd. I know they are going to love you, but it might take them a little while to realize that, okay?" Solomon blew a rush of air through his nostrils. Jodi did the same.

"You're home," she said, rubbing her hand along his neck.

Tania and another volunteer named Amanda walked toward Jodi.

"Can we say hi?" Tania asked.

Jodi waved them over. "Of course!"

As Jodi introduced two of her most faithful and capable volunteers to Solomon, she noticed Ty talking to Jessica and Richard on the office porch. They both laughed at something their dad said. Ty was so much better at keeping things light and fun with them. Jodi wished she could be more like that, but most days she felt anything but light and fun. While Tania and Amanda fussed over Solomon, commenting on the red hue of his chestnut coat, Jodi noticed Richard kick the bottom of the porch railing and shake his head. A moment later, Jessica shook her head apologetically. Then the two walked to the house. Ty cast a look of regret at Jodi. *Guess they weren't interested in participating after all.*

How did we get to this point? she wondered for the hundredth time. Three years ago, Jodi had envisioned she and her family working together to help people find hope and healing. That vision kept her going when things got hard—when she discovered just how much time and money it takes to run a horse ranch; how much experience she did *not* have; and how emotionally draining it was to step out of her comfort zone and ask people to donate their money, time, and talents to make her dream a reality. But every time she thought about quitting, she pictured her family working together to bring hope and light to their community, and she pressed on.

At first, they did press on together—working as a team to build fences, clear brush, and prepare their unused acreage for horses. It had been hard, exhausting work, but it was healing work for Jodi. She thought that was true for Ty and the kids too.

The day their first horse arrived, Jessica cheered and Richard helped Ty unload the white horse. But as four more horses were added to the farm, and HopeWell moved from a fun family project to a time-consuming, life-altering reality, Jodi's idyllic vision began to evaporate like a mirage. The more time she devoted to HopeWell, the less time her children did. And when they were told to help with farm chores, they would sigh or roll their eyes. After six months, the excitement of starting a brand-new adventure had turned into nothing more than a burden-some chore to Jessica and Richard.

In some ways Jodi understood. After all, in less than a year she had gone from a full-time homeschooling mom to a full-time therapy ranch manager, who somehow still managed to oversee homeschooling. Surely her kids missed the way things used to be. *But couldn't they see all the good they were doing at HopeWell?*

Jodi got a lump in her throat as she watched Jessica and Richard disappear into the house. It had become a safe haven for her kids, the one place on the property where they could be alone.

Jodi realized that maybe she did need to establish better boundaries for herself between home life and HopeWell life. But with so many people needing her time and attention, and with most of them in tremendous emotional pain, how could she possibly turn them away?

Jodi shook off her worries; they would still be there tomorrow. Today, Solomon needed to be corralled in his temporary field.

Ty walked up to Jodi and put his arm around her. "You ready to show this guy to his room?"

"Absolutely."

Jodi clicked her tongue and started walking Solomon toward the small field across from the office. She kept a slow pace, allowing him to pull at the grass. When they finally arrived at their destination, Ty held the gate while Jodi escorted Solomon through the opening. He confidently entered the field, then froze. His nostrils expanded as he took in the scents of his new environment—especially those of his curious new neighbors across the wire fence.

"Well, what do you think?" Jodi asked, running her fingers through Solomon's mane.

His tail flicked a pesky fly away as he pounded the ground with his hoof. He approached the equine receiving line as Jodi introduced everyone to him.

"Our beautiful mares are at the far end of the fence line. Miracle is the chestnut. She's the oldest mare—and a friend to anyone who comes through our gates. The two black-and-white beauties standing next to her are Destiny and her mom, Lady. Many of our boys are quite smitten with those two," Jodi informed Solomon with a chuckle.

Solomon raised and lowered his head several times in rapid succession, tearing off clumps of grass. *Horse stress eating*. After several minutes, Solomon raised his head and took several more steps toward the fence. Jodi followed, holding his lead line loosely in her hand.

She continued the introductions. "The horse on the end closest to us is Beau—he's such a good boy, just like you. He even looks a little bit like you, doesn't he? We think he's part Tennessee walking horse. Then there's Justice. He's a mustang and can be quite a handful. But I bet you two will be good buddies. Next is Opie. He's been at the bottom of the pecking order for quite a while, so he's probably really glad you're here."

Jodi hoped Opie wouldn't fight too hard to move up the chain of command. "Then there's—" Jodi was interrupted by an ear-piercing bray. Solomon's head shot up, trying to pinpoint where the sound was coming from.

"Well, I guess Bubba Jack got tired of waiting his turn." Jodi laughed, shaking her head at the precocious gray-and-white donkey standing between the mares and the other geldings. "Bubba Jack is quite the character, and he will be your friend for life." Solomon had paused during Bubba Jack's interjection, but he slowly began to move forward once again until they were within ten feet of the fence.

"The horse beside Opie is Samson. The kids call him Surfer Boy because of his long blond mane. But don't let his nickname fool you. He's a pretty calm and quiet boy, and he's great with the kids. And then finally, there's Victory," Jodi said, smiling at one of her most beloved horses. "He is the head honcho around here. Oh, and he's a quarter horse like you! Victory is also the oldest horse out here and a very good leader."

Victory let out a whinny, making sure the newcomer knew who was in charge. Solomon's head shot up, his ears back. Victory turned sideways, showing off his size. Solomon stepped back, acknowledging Victory's display of dominance. After walking Solomon around the perimeter of his temporary field and then stopping at the water trough and hay box, Jodi removed his halter and turned him loose.

"I'll be back in a bit to feed you dinner," Jodi promised.

The volunteers had already hung a hay bag, but Jodi would return in a few hours to distribute the horses' evening feed and supplements. Ty opened the gate as Jodi approached.

"How's Solomon doing?"

"I think he's doing okay," Jodi said. "Coping with a little stress eating."

"What an excellent idea!" Ty exclaimed, putting his arm across his wife's shoulders. "I think we should do a little bit of that ourselves. What's for lunch?"

When they got to the farmhouse, Ty stopped to remove his shoes while Jodi went inside to check on the kids. Jessica and Richard were watching television in the family room.

"Have you guys eaten yet?"

Richard pointed to a plate with evidence of grape jelly and a few potato chip crumbs.

"I'm not hungry," Jessica said.

The hot water from the sink felt heavenly on Jodi's hands. She put some leftover chili in the microwave to warm up, and then she walked back into the family room.

"Thank you both for coming out to see Solomon. It was really nice to have you there."

"He looks like a good horse," Richard said.

"Well, if you want to meet him later, you can come with me this evening when I feed him. No one else will be there."

"Maybe . . . ," Richard mumbled.

Swallowing a heavy sigh, Jodi returned to the kitchen just as the microwave beeped and Ty walked in. They sat at the small kitchen table, with Jodi getting up every few minutes to look out the window and check on Solomon, who was watching Beau and Victory running along the fence line.

"I need to meet with Tania after lunch to discuss a new child who's coming out next week," Jodi told Ty as she washed out her bowl.

"I'll leave you to that, and I'll get to my route," he said.

How Ty managed to keep a full-time job as a mail carrier and help her run the ranch was an utter mystery, but an incredible blessing. She was tired enough from one job. No wonder the poor man could barely make it through a movie without falling asleep.

"You have more HopeWell work to do today?" Jessica called out from the family room. "You said you would take me to get new shoes for Sunday. My boots are too small. And we can't go tomorrow because I'm going to Casey's birthday party." Jessica walked into the kitchen and stared at her mother. "You forgot, didn't you?"

Jodi's shoulders drooped. She had forgotten about their shopping date. She checked her watch. *If I meet with Tania now and move my calls to Monday, then I could take Jessica shopping and still get back here in time to feed the horses.*

"Of course, I didn't forget," she fibbed. "I just need to meet with Tania for a few minutes, and then we can go. Why don't you eat something while I'm gone so you can be ready as soon as I get back?"

Jessica looked skeptically at her mom but nodded.

Within twenty minutes, Jodi had managed to get everything set with Tania for the new child's arrival, rearranged Monday's schedule to allow for two hours of phone calls to donors, and made an appointment with their veterinarian, Dr. Pol, to give Solomon a thorough examination.

The drive to the mall had been quiet, with Jessica giving one-word replies to Jodi's questions about her day. But by the time they walked into the second shoe store, the teenager's mood had lifted, and mother and daughter shared laughs and easy conversation while they searched for the perfect shoes. After trying on at least ten pairs, Jessica finally decided on a cute pair of "church boots" as she called them. Once they returned home, Jessica helped Jodi with dinner while Richard set the table. Jodi was just setting their casserole on the table when Ty walked in the back door.

"Smells delicious," he said, hanging his coat on the hook.

Jodi ate quickly, anxious to check on Solomon and aware that the herd was waiting for their own dinner.

"You guys can come meet Solomon after you help your dad clean up the kitchen," Jodi called out while walking to the back door.

She couldn't make out any intelligible words from the grunts and mumbles coming from the table.

After delivering nine large bowls filled with grain and various supplements to the horses, Jodi stood with Solomon. The pale sky would soon give way to darkness.

"Guess the kids had other things to do." She sighed, running her hand along the horse's back. "Don't be offended. It's not you. It's me."

Solomon set his large chin on Jodi's shoulder and exhaled.

"If only they could experience this place like I have," she continued as if talking to a friend. She reached up to stroke the side of his face. "This place—the people, the animals—all of it . . . it's . . ." Her voice caught in her throat as fear and loneliness settled over her, but she quickly shook it off.

"They'll come around one day," she declared. "Won't they?" She wasn't sure if she was asking the horse, herself, or God. But Jodi hoped someone would answer.

3

THE NEXT MORNING Jodi was up well before sunrise, anxious to check on Solomon. She moved as quietly as possible down the hallway, hoping not to step on a squeaky floorboard and wake her kids. Of course, Jodi often joked that if the horses were to stampede through their bedrooms, Jessica and Richard would sleep right through it.

After a quick breakfast of toast and coffee, Jodi donned her early winter gear—a puffy coat, fleece hat, work gloves, and boots—and headed out the back door. Traverse, the family's yellow lab mix, followed closely behind. The sky had brightened just enough to forgo a flashlight.

Jodi headed toward the large pasture in the middle of their property. She loved walking around the ranch at this time in the morning. Everything was so quiet, so peaceful. There was no loud equipment running and no people clamoring for her attention. She could just make out the equine silhouettes in the distance. Many of the animals were still asleep. It was her chance to breathe in the tranquility of the ranch, to steady herself for the day's events, and to spend a few uninterrupted moments with God in prayer.

These prayer walks had become a wonderful routine for her, an interlude before the day got underway. To pray for those who would come through the HopeWell gate that day—the volunteers and those they would serve—for the ever-growing needs of the ranch; for her family; and for the many animals in her care. She loved HopeWell and was honored to be a part of something so important. But the truth was . . .

A loud bray ricocheted through the quiet ranch. "I'm coming, I'm coming," Jodi called back. *No time to get lost in your thoughts when an impatient donkey is hungry.* "But you need to wait a few minutes," she said. "I need to check on someone first."

"Good morning, Solomon." He was half-dozing in the small field. "How was your first night?"

Solomon's ears turned toward Jodi, and then he headed in her direction.

When he got to the fence, he nudged her shoulder and exhaled loudly. Jodi leaned against his muzzle and breathed out her own greeting.

"Good morning, sweet one."

Victory whinnied, causing Solomon to step back several paces.

"All right, all right," Jodi said, putting her hands up in mock surrender toward Victory. "I will go and get your breakfast. Goodness, you all are grumpy when you're hungry."

For the next hour, Jodi filled hay boxes, prepared and delivered bowls of grain and supplements, and topped off water troughs. She continued to pray as she worked—for Solomon to adjust quickly and for emotional healing for those who came to HopeWell today. "And God, thank you once again for choosing me to start HopeWell. You knew how much I needed it, and you promised to be with me."

She inhaled deeply. "When a promise from God is all you have, then you live like it's all you need," she said aloud, feeling more determined to keep following wherever he led.

As she pushed the empty wheelbarrow back to the feed shed, Ty came around the corner.

"Hey there, early bird. Did you leave any work for the rest of us?"

"I wanted to check on Solomon, and once the herd saw me, they decided it was breakfast time." Jodi shoved her hands into her pockets and wished she had thought to put hand warmers in there. "Besides, keeping busy helps me stay warm."

An hour later, several volunteers arrived to continue construction on the arena. As the small team worked throughout the morning, Jodi kept an eye on Solomon, who kept his eye on the herd. Victory, Samson, and Justice patrolled the fence line like guards doing double time at the Tomb of the Unknown Soldier. Occasional whinnies and nickers volleyed back and forth between the herd and Solomon. And in the middle of the field, running, bucking, and at times twirling, was Bubba Jack. The little donkey seemed determined to display his dominance. His antics fell short of the aggressive behavior he was undoubtedly going for. But he managed to entertain the volunteers and confuse Solomon.

Jodi enjoyed a quick lunch under the pavilion with Tania, Amanda, and Ty as they discussed the timeline for moving Solomon into the large field.

"He seems ready to me," Tania said assuredly.

Jodi studied Solomon standing nose to nose at the fence with Lady. There was no doubt Solomon was ready to officially join the herd. The real question was this: Was the herd ready for Solomon?

U

A week later, Solomon was turned out into the pasture with the rest of the herd. Within minutes, an explosive, high-pitched whinny got everyone's attention. Like a starter's pistol at a race, Victory's signal set everyone in motion. Solomon broke into a run, with the other horses chasing him. Bubba Jack brought up the rear. The sight of nine running horses would have been beautiful—majestic even—if it weren't so terrifying. Jodi had planned to move Solomon into the pasture the week before, but between unrelenting rains and suffering from a miserable head cold, she had delayed it. Jodi chewed her lip as she watched the massive game of chase.

Why isn't introducing horses to each other as easy as introducing a child to a new preschool class? A shared toy, some Goldfish crackers and juice boxes, and usually the kids became instant friends. Preschoolers didn't run full speed toward each other, then turn around and kick with all their might. And if they did bite—which Jodi was grateful her kids never did—it wasn't with close to five hundred pounds of pressure per square inch!

Jodi was grateful she had gloves on. Otherwise, her tight fists would have left marks on her palms.

"They're fine," Ty tried to reassure her.

One look at her husband and Jodi knew that he was also trying to reassure himself.

"Good thing you got out of there when you did," Tania said.

"It's like catch and release," Jodi mused. "Catch the horse in the small field, then release him fast in the big one."

The herd—with Solomon in the lead—galloped past the three spectators, their hooves sounding like rolling thunder.

"Oh, I hope they don't catch him," Jodi fretted.

She hated seeing the horses she loved so much—horses who did such good work—kick and bite and strike each other. Still, she knew it was nature's way, a God-given instinct. But she really wished God had given them more of a *hug it out* instinct.

All Jodi could do was stand back and watch. She would only intervene if things got truly dangerous. Of course, when she first started HopeWell, she had considered this herd behavior dangerous. Thankfully, the team she had assembled to help her get the ranch up and running had helped her learn to read horse mannerisms and better interpret their behavior. As a result, her tolerance for these types of stress-inducing interactions had increased. But this was still one of the least pleasant parts of her job.

As suddenly as the horse race had begun, it ended. Victory was the first to stop. The mares veered off to the right and stood together, their ears pointed toward Solomon. As Beau, Justice, and Samson slowed from a gallop to a trot, Solomon turned left and halted, his tail brushing up against the fence. Bubba Jack, either oblivious to the fact that his herd leader had stopped or simply not wanting the game to end, continued running in large circles around the other horses. Solomon glanced curiously at Bubba Jack, then focused again on the herd standing twenty feet away.

After pausing for a moment to sniff the air, Opie began walking slowly toward Solomon. His black-ringed ears were flattened, his chin tucked, his eyes wide. Solomon's ears shot forward, and his nostrils flared. He leaned his head away from Opie's approach. Jodi knew what was coming a moment before it did. Once Opie got within a few feet of Solomon, he whipped around and kicked. Jodi couldn't tell if he made contact. Solomon returned a half-hearted kick, then sidestepped several paces.

Reveling in the fact that he got the larger horse to move, Opie pranced back to his herd. His tail was so high he looked as if he were in a parade. Minutes later, order was restored as the horses spread out in the pasture and began grazing. Jodi took advantage of the brief reprieve to take a deep breath and fill her lungs with the crisp morning air. After two days of cold drizzle, the bright blue sky was a welcome sight—even with temperatures near freezing.

"Since the herd appears to have called a temporary truce, what do you ladies say to a coffee break?" Ty asked.

"I say your brilliance is one of the many reasons I married you," Jodi replied.

"How about bringing me coffee when you come back?" Tania said. "I'll stay here and keep an eye on everybody."

"Your takeout order will be ready in a few minutes," Jodi assured Tania. "A whole thermos full." Just before heading inside the office building, Jodi glanced toward the field. At that exact moment, Beau swung around toward Solomon and kicked.

Ugh. Where are Goldfish crackers and juice boxes when you need them?

Three hours and two cups of coffee later, Jodi stood outside the pasture. But this time her thoughts were on the little boy who had just left the ranch.

"I feel so bad for Shawn," Jodi said to Linda, a psychotherapist who volunteered her time at HopeWell. "I just don't know how to best serve that little guy. Last week he didn't connect with Beau or with Lady. I really thought Bubba Jack would be a good match for him today. I mean, Bubba Jack is normally a good match for everyone."

Linda looked thoughtfully at the donkey, who grazed contentedly between them on a lead line.

"I just don't think Bubba Jack knows what to do with Shawn's energy—or with his unpredictability," Linda observed. "I think Shawn's outburst and loud vocalizations make Bubba Jack feel on edge. Shawn then seems to sense—and maybe even internalize—Bubba's response, and it agitates him further. And the cycle continues."

"The horses have never worked with someone so severely impacted by autism," Jodi said. "And I'm not sure how to even begin to train them to help kids like Shawn. I guess we could try desensitizing them more to loud human sounds and sudden movements?"

She and Linda spent the next twenty minutes in the pavilion discussing supplemental training for some of the horses. In the meantime, they would let Shawn spend time with the bunnies, hoping that the smaller animals might be a better fit for the boy.

When they were done, they continued to watch the chase-the-new-guy game in the field.

"Poor Solomon," Jodi murmured. "He must be exhausted. Actually, they all must be. They've run themselves ragged out of fear—unnecessary fear."

"As you've told me many times," Linda said, "the herd needs to build trust with the newest member, and this is part of that process. This is how the new horse learns the dynamics of his new herd, right? Give them time. They'll figure it out."

Jodi appreciated Linda's calm, cool presence, as well as her concrete approach to problems. As a mental health therapist and a knowledgeable horse owner herself, Linda understood both the nuances of equine behavior and the struggles of the human heart.

Jodi knew the antics in the pasture were normal. *Why am I so on edge this time? Why am I so protective of Solomon?*

She pondered those questions during her morning chores around the ranch and as she worked in the office. She pondered them while preparing lunch for her kids and after reviewing their homeschool reports on the Titanic. And she was still thinking of them that evening when she and two volunteers fed all of the HopeWell animals.

When the chores were done and Jodi said goodnight to the volunteers, she gazed at Solomon. He looked so eager and hopeful to be a part of the herd. And yet so alone. Did he miss Ken and Sue? Did he miss his plastic deer friend? "God, why am I getting so upset over Solomon's adjustment?"

She waited for an answer, some inner knowledge to suddenly come to mind.

Nothing came.

Instead, Jessica called out to her from between their home and the HopeWell office. "Mom! Dad said that dinner's ready! Are you coming?"

"Be right there."

She turned back to the horses. "Please try and get along, okay? You need each other. And I need you to figure this out—the sooner the better."

One of the horses whinnied. Solomon turned his head in Jodi's direction.

"Hang in there, boy," she mumbled. "It will get better . . . I hope."

Jodi squared her shoulders and took a deep breath. She couldn't afford to fall apart. Too many people were depending on her.

"Get it together, Jodi," she scolded herself.

She pushed the wheelbarrow back to the hay barn, secured the door, and headed to the house. Ty and the kids were laughing when she entered the kitchen.

"You look like you're having fun. What's so funny?"

"Just something Dad said," Jessica explained. "You had to be here to get it."

Ouch.

"Well, dinner smells great," Jodi said, trying to sound upbeat.

A feeling of loneliness began to squeeze her heart like a vise as she ate dinner. She listened to everyone's stories, nodding and smiling in all the right places. She tried sharing a little about her day, specifically about Solomon's adjustment—or rather his lack thereof. Jessica and Richard half-listened, and although Ty seemed genuinely interested, he couldn't hide his yawns.

They don't care. Why should they? The ranch was her dream.

And any issues were ultimately hers to figure out. As Jodi began clearing the dishes, Ty got up to help.

"I've got it," she assured him. "You cooked. I'll clean."

"You're the best," he said.

"I know," she lied.

Ty headed to his workshop to putter, and Jodi shooed the kids upstairs to finish their schoolwork. As she stood in the quiet kitchen, she stared out the window toward the large field. Everything was swallowed by the darkness, other than the glow of the back porch light. Was Solomon still standing far from the others? Would he ever feel like part of the herd?

Jodi scrubbed a pan vigorously until her fingertips were wrinkled like raisins and the pan was sparkling clean.

4

THE NEXT MORNING DAWNED BRIGHT AND CLEAR, both on the ranch and within Jodi's heart. The lonely darkness of the previous night gave way to the brightness of a day filled with new possibilities. "God, thank you for protecting the animals through the night," Jodi said, chatting aloud with God as she did her chores. "Please let the horses adjust quickly to Solomon and help him adjust to being here." Jodi paused to fill the chicken feeder and top off their water. As she exited the gate of their enclosure, her prayers turned toward her children. "God, please help me connect with Jessica and Richard when they come by later to help me decorate the ranch. I'm so glad they agreed to do it again this year, but I'm so worried I'll say something wrong or do something wrong."

The kids were still sleeping when she had left this morning, so she had left a note reminding them to come and help after they completed their morning schoolwork.

Suddenly, a feeling of unease washed over her. *What if they don't want to come? Should I make them?* This was supposed to be a fun event—a way to connect and enjoy the ranch together. But recently so many things she thought would be fun just ended up driving her and her kids further apart. She was so wrapped up in her thoughts, she didn't even realize that she had arrived at the pasture.

"Hello again," Jodi greeted the herd. "I guess now that you've eaten your grain and oats, you're ready for some hay, huh?"

A medley of nickers and whinnies gave her the answer. Jodi opened the gate and pushed the wheelbarrow inside. She deposited several flakes of hay in the boxes scattered throughout the field. Victory—as always—took the first mouthful, followed by Beau, Justice, Miracle, Samson, Lady, Destiny, Opie, and then—in a league all his own—Bubba Jack. Standing far behind the little donkey, in the middle of the field watching everyone eat, was Solomon. His ears were forward, his posture relaxed, his head facing the herd. Jodi grabbed two handfuls of hay from the box she had just filled and walked over to him.

"Oh, sweet boy," she said, "I'm sorry you're not a part of the group yet."

As Solomon took the hay from her hand, the whiskers on his chin tickled her palm, while a memory of her own loneliness surfaced. A painful memory Jodi kept buried, but one that was as much a part of her as her love for horses and her desire to help hurting people.

"Can I tell you a secret?" Jodi quietly asked. "I know how

much it hurts to be rejected. It makes everything feel dark. Hopeless." Jodi looked past Solomon to the trees in the distance. But her heart went all the way back to her adolescent years, when an all-consuming first love ended in a painful breakup and set off a chain reaction of depression and despair.

"I was so desperate to be loved that I gave up a part of myself. I lost that relationship, and I lost myself."

Jodi paused. She inhaled a shaky breath and stroked Solomon's neck. "I stopped interacting with people. I stopped feeling joy. And at some point . . . whether to punish myself or to try to gain some kind of control over something in my life . . . I just stopped eating."

As if needing to assure Solomon that he didn't need to worry about deprivation, she handed him another handful of hay before continuing. "Eventually, people started to notice. My parents, my teachers. They saw that I was wasting away. That's when they enrolled me in 4-H. I guess they hoped taking care of animals would help me take care of myself." For a moment, she went back in her mind's eye to how she had spent every waking hour learning to care for bunnies, before working with and giving her heart to horses.

Solomon bumped Jodi's shoulder with his muzzle, bringing her back to the present. Jodi was out of hay, but she gladly offered him a back scratch. "You know, looking back, I can see how God used that 4-H program to lead my heart to him. I didn't know him . . . wasn't even looking for him, but he saw me. Just like he saw you and brought you here."

Horses are so much easier to talk to than people. Jodi shooed several flies away from her confidant and whispered, "You are loved, Solomon. Whether you feel it or not, and whether or not the herd shows it, I promise you are loved. You are wanted. And your presence here matters."

Jodi let her hand trail down Solomon's back and rested her head against his neck. As she breathed in the scents of horses, hay, and morning air, she felt the words she had just spoken to Solomon being whispered to her own heart.

You are loved.

You are wanted.

You matter.

Solomon's nostrils were in front of Jodi's face. He exhaled. She exhaled and leaned her forehead against the thin white stripe on his muzzle. Jodi heard the rest of the herd chewing and felt the cold breeze on her face. But she focused on Solomon. For some reason, he evoked powerful emotions from her, feelings she tried so hard to keep hidden away from everyone—herself most of all. Jodi heard one car door shut, two, three—the volunteers had arrived. It was time to pull herself together, put a smile on her face, and get to work. She gave Solomon one last scratch.

"Don't let them bully you too much. You have just as much right to be here as they do; that hay is just as much yours as theirs."

As she pushed the wheelbarrow through the gate, Solomon moved to the hay box that Bubba Jack and Opie had just left. Solomon managed to take a few mouthfuls before Opie nudged him out of the way.

Several hours later, Jessica and Richard walked into the HopeWell office. Jodi and Linda had been reviewing plans for a tour they would be facilitating later that afternoon for a group of third graders. Just two weeks earlier, an eight-year-old girl named Haley had died of complications following a routine surgery. Haley's teacher, Mrs. Jefferis, had reached out to Jodi several days after the little girl's death to see if HopeWell might be willing to host some of her students.

"I'm just hoping to provide a safe place for them to begin to process their grief," she had said on the phone. Jodi had heard the heartbreaking story beforehand from friends. She emailed the necessary permission forms to Mrs. Jefferis for the children's parents and guardians to sign. Jodi knew that one session with a horse wouldn't magically make everything better. But she did know—both from seeing it happen many times and from experiencing it firsthand—that spending time with horses, especially those trained for therapeutic work, could help people begin to process and heal from a wide array of hurts and losses. She hoped that would be the case for the seven children coming to the ranch. And with the weather getting colder by the minute, she was thankful the covered arena was far enough along in construction to allow them to host the session inside.

Jodi waved Jessica and Richard into her office.

"Hi, guys! I'm so glad you are here," she said, beaming. "Ms. Linda and I were just finishing up our meeting."

Linda greeted Jessica and Richard with a warm smile and comments about how quickly they were growing. Jodi watched her children as they spoke with Linda. *When did Jessica develop such poise? When did Richard's jaw become so angular?* They really were growing up fast—too fast. Four years ago they were her little man and her little princess. *Four years ago they were all so happy. Four years ago they were . . .*

An unexpected wave of grief hit like a tsunami. Jodi gripped the back of a chair. She commanded herself to ride out the pain until she could force it back down. Thankfully, Linda had the kids talking about their favorite Thanksgiving foods and what size Christmas tree they were hoping for this year.

"Well . . . my Thanksgiving elves," Jodi said, a few minutes later, her voice tight but her emotions more stable. "Are you ready to help me bring some festive cheer to the ranch?"

"I don't think Thanksgiving elves are a thing," Jessica said with the perfect mix of teenage exasperation and childlike amusement.

"I think we *should* make it a thing then," Jodi replied, as excitement pushed away grief.

She pulled a Santa hat out of one bin of decorations and a cardboard turkey cut-out from another. She tucked the turkey into the fold of the hat and placed it on Richard's head.

"See! A Thanksgiving elf!" she said with a laugh.

Jessica tried to suppress a giggle, but when Richard began to gobble to the tune of "Jingle Bells" she couldn't help but laugh. Laughing with her kids was a gift. *How long has it been since we've shared a belly laugh?* Jodi couldn't remember.

"I think Thanksgiving elves are perfect since we are decorating for both Thanksgiving and Christmas," Jodi said. "We don't want to pass over Thanksgiving and all it stands for, so we'll decorate the office and the exterior of some of our buildings with reminders to give thanks. But since our Christmas open house is next week, we'll go ahead and decorate for that as well."

Richard and Jessica nodded. They knew that when hosting an outdoor Christmas event in central Michigan, any time after Halloween is acceptable.

After dividing the decorations into three piles, Jodi made two more Thanksgiving elf hats, and the three of them set to work. They hung "Give Thanks" and "Thankful" signs around the office, secured two harvest-themed wreaths on the feed and tack room doors, and created an enchanting display beside the covered pavilion using hay bales, apple crates, and several plastic pumpkins. For the upcoming Christmas open house, Jessica and Richard decorated an artificial Christmas tree, which would be stored inside the HopeWell office until the event. They also hung several strings of garland and Christmas lights around the pavilion.

"Good job, my fellow elves," Jodi said two hours later, as they sat on top of a picnic table admiring their work. "We managed to pull off a very festive look."

"It really does look good," Jessica agreed. "I think Thanksgiving and Christmas decorations look good together. We should make Thanksgivingmas a thing!"

Richard agreed, looking at Jodi excitedly. "We could fill a giant cornucopia with Christmas treats and desserts!"

"That sounds delicious!" she agreed, before adding, "but then all the animals will want to break out of their enclosures to raid the cornucopia! Can you imagine Bubba Jack with chocolate? It would be complete mayhem out here. You might start a stampede."

"Sounds fun to me!" Richard laughed, petting one of the many stray cats who had found its way to HopeWell.

This moment felt so good. So natural. So . . . normal.

"How is Solomon doing?"

Wait! Jessica is asking about one of the horses? Wow! Play it cool, Jodi.

"Pretty good, I think. Although he is struggling a bit to fit in," she answered honestly. "The herd still isn't so sure about him, but he's hanging in there. I just wish they would hurry up and invite him in."

Jessica's expression was thoughtful.

"Do you think he wishes he hadn't come here?" the teenager asked softly.

Jodi looked toward the field, but the horses were out of sight, probably grazing on the far side of the pasture.

"I hope not," Jodi answered. "Even though he was greatly loved, he was really lonely where he was. I think . . . I hope," she clarified, "that even though he's still on the outs with the herd, the hope of a community is better than no community at all."

Jessica stared toward the field.

"I think . . . ," she began.

"Jodi, Mrs. Jefferis just phoned," Amanda, who had recently started working as an administrative assistant, called from the office porch. "Eight more children have permission forms and want to come out this afternoon. So we'll have a total of fifteen. She asked if you could call her back to discuss a few things before they arrive."

Several thoughts buzzed through Jodi's mind simultaneously:

We just doubled the size of today's group.

We need to rethink some logistics.

What was Jessica about to say?

Jodi's heart sank as she saw her daughter's posture shift.

"No problem, Amanda. I'll stop by before the kids and I head home for lunch."

Jodi turned back to her daughter. "Sorry, sweetheart, what were you going to say?"

"Oh, nothing," Jessica said, dismissing the conversation with a wave. "Come on, Richard. We should get back to our schoolwork."

"I'm sorry, guys. This large group of kids coming out tonight recently lost—"

"We know you're busy with important stuff, Mom. We can make our own lunch," Jessica said, as she started walking to the house.

Richard followed his sister, but he called back to his mom, "Think about the cornucopia idea! Everyone would love it!"

Jodi's half-hearted chuckle quickly faded when she noticed the two discarded Thanksgiving elf hats sitting on the picnic table. She added hers to the pile.

After returning Mrs. Jefferis's phone call, Jodi texted Linda the change: *We're splitting the large group of children into two smaller groups.* She then walked home to grab a late lunch and check on Jessica and Richard. Hopefully, they really had understood why she needed to go. She hated feeling as though she had to choose between her kids and the ranch so often. She tried so hard to be everything for everyone. And yet she constantly felt like she was letting everyone down. It wasn't supposed to be this way. Her kids were supposed to be as involved with HopeWell as she was. That had been the plan at the beginning. When had that changed? How had the place that brought her such hope—that offered such hope to so many—become a source of contention with her children?

The house was quiet when she entered. "Jessica? Richard? You guys upstairs?"

"I am," Richard answered. "I'm finishing my math work. I think Jess is on the porch."

"I'll be up to check it in a bit."

She found Jessica buried under a pile of blankets on the glider in the corner of their screened porch.

"Whatcha doing out here?" Jodi asked softly. "Aren't you cold?"

"I'm fine," Jessica answered without taking her eyes from the book in her hands.

"Can I get you anything while I heat up my lunch?"

"Nope. I'm fine."

Jodi wasn't giving up. "What are you reading?"

"*Wuthering Heights.*"

"I remember reading that in school," Jodi said. "It was good, but kind of depressing, right?"

"I like it."

Several silent minutes ticked by before Jodi finally broke it.

"Sweetheart, you were about to tell me something earlier when Amanda interrupted. Will you tell me what you were about to say?"

Jodi bit her bottom lip as Jessica folded down the page corner of her book and adjusted her blankets.

"I don't remember."

"Jess, I think you do. And I think it was important to you. Would you please tell me?"

"You don't have to talk to me like I'm one of your HopeWell kids. I'm fine. I was just curious about Solomon, that's all. It's no big deal."

Jessica stood up and gathered the blankets in her arms.

"I am getting cold. I'm going to finish reading in my room."

As Jodi watched her daughter leave, her heart ached. *God, why does it have to be so hard? Talking with Jessica used to be as easy as breathing. Am I losing her?*

Where did that thought come from? I haven't lost Jessica. Jessica is a teenager, and moodiness is just part of the deal.

It had been for Jodi. In fact, her love of horses, and her knowledge of how they could help a hurting heart, had come about during her own teenage years—when the angst and drama of her first broken heart had started to consume her. Jodi often told people later that the horses had pointed her to God—even though she didn't know that's who she was seeing at the time. The way the horses sought out her company and didn't care what she looked like or had done, but just wanted to be with her, that planted a seed in her heart. A seed of a thought that maybe—just maybe—she was worth being around. One day, many years later, that seed sprouted roots when she was introduced to a kind and good God who loved her enough to put horses on this earth to point her to him.

Jodi finished her lunch, reviewed Richard's algebra work—thankful for the teacher's book that contained all the answers—and checked on Jessica, who was lost on the moors of *Wuthering Heights*. She then returned to the HopeWell office to make some follow-up calls and review paperwork for several new clients who had reached out for services. They likely would only be able to get in one visit before the weather turned too cold and the ranch closed for the season.

After finishing her last phone call, she glanced up at the clock. "Four o'clock already?" She noticed the "Be Thankful" sign Richard had hung on her door earlier that day and smiled.

Just then, Linda and Amanda walked into the office. "Oh, it

feels nice in here!" Linda said, shutting the door quickly against the biting wind. "Do you think the kids will want to play board games in here instead of interacting with the horses?"

"Not a chance," Jodi said, with a laugh.

The three women grabbed the halters and lead ropes they would need, then headed on to the pasture to get Bubba Jack, Opie, Samson, and Lady. Jodi lagged behind as they approached the field, glancing toward the house. She hadn't meant to stay in the office so long. Ty should be getting home soon. She knew he would handle things at home, but a pang of guilt assaulted her. She was the mom. She should be the one handling things at home, right? She indulged in a weary sigh before focusing on the task at hand. The women had no problems corraling the four horses they would be working with. They led them to the arena where they removed the halters and lead ropes and allowed the horses to be at liberty while waiting for the children to arrive.

Several minutes later, Jodi heard a large vehicle turn into the gravel driveway. As she walked out of the arena to greet their visitors, a group of children started running toward her.

"Look over there! By that fence—real-life horses!" a little girl shouted.

Jodi's heart swelled with joy and compassion. Yes, her own children needed her, and they would always be her priority. But these little ones needed her too. They needed HopeWell and the healing it could offer them.

5

As JODI GREETED Mrs. Jefferis and the children, she recognized a familiar face.

"Hi, Shontell," Jodi said.

Shontell's brown eyes beamed at Jodi.

"Haley was my friend," Shontell stated. "She played with me at recess. But she died, and now we can't play anymore."

Jodi's heart broke for the little girl who had experienced such loss in her young life—including the loss of the only home and family she had known when her mother was arrested and imprisoned. And now her friend Haley. Jodi longed to cuddle the little girl and hide her away from any further pain. If only that were possible.

"Oh, honey, I am so sorry you lost your friend."

"Can I see the horses?" Shontell asked.

"You sure can! You get to see lots of horses today."

Shontell's face lit up, the sadness of a moment ago giving way to pure joy. Jodi felt a pang of envy, unsure of whether she was reacting to Shontell's ability to compartmentalize her grief, or of her ability to own it. But she didn't have time to figure it out. Jodi welcomed everyone and gave them a brief introduction to the ranch before dividing them in two groups and assigning each group to a leader, who would introduce them to the HopeWell animals. The goal of the group session was to provide a safe environment for the children to share—if they wanted to. No one would force them to talk. The focus of the session was simply being present with them. The children would be allowed to set the pace.

It had already been decided that Jodi would remain in the arena where she would introduce the children to the four horses inside the fence. Shontell's group headed outside with Linda to meet the bunnies, while Amanda's group started in the arena. The look on the children's faces as the horses approached was priceless. Several of the children's eyes grew wide, others' mouths dropped open, and a few tilted their heads back as Samson and Opie leaned over the wooden rail. The authentic expressions of awe and joy the children showed when meeting the herd always tugged at Jodi's heart. But for some reason, today she felt sad. Bubba Jack nudged her shoulder from inside the gate. *My adoring public is here to see me, not watch you sort through your feelings*, his not-so-gentle head bump seemed to say.

"Manners please, Bubba Jack," Jodi corrected, applying firm pressure to his chest to get him to take several steps back. "They may be here to see you, but that is no excuse for bad manners."

Bubba Jack took two very slow and deliberate steps back, then let out an ear-piercing bray. Several of the children covered their ears. A few jumped. One little boy imitated the sound—throwing his head back and yelling out his own *hee-haw*. Bubba Jack was in heaven! He answered right back, which caused a chorus of *hee-haws* and laughter to fill the arena. Leave it to their resident goofball of a donkey to give a group of grieving children the gift of laughter. Bad manners forgiven, Jodi kissed the top of Bubba Jack's head, then proceeded to tell the children about their new equine friends and share a few of their stories.

"Bubba Jack and Samson came from the same farm up north."

One little boy looked at Jodi with a sad expression on his face and asked, "Did their other owners not want them anymore?"

Jodi crouched to look the boy in the eyes.

"The people who were taking care of Bubba Jack and Samson had to move to a smaller house, and they didn't have space for them anymore. When they found out about HopeWell, they thought it would be a good place for their animal friends to live. They wanted Bubba Jack and Samson to be able to help other people's hearts feel happy, just like they made their hearts feel happy while they had them."

Jodi motioned to the bay-colored Arabian wandering around the arena. As if on cue, Opie stopped and looked over at Jodi and the group of enthralled children.

"That's Opie," she said, pointing to the small, fine-boned horse. "Can anyone tell me what letter you see on his face?"

Little hands shot up in the air. Jodi chose a petite girl, with a head full of curls. "T," she answered softly.

"That's right!"

"How did Opie get here?" a curious young voice asked.

"Opie was left at a farm when his owner moved away," Jodi explained. "He was found and rescued by a very kind woman who owned a boarding facility—a special farm where horses stay. She kept Opie there until she found out about HopeWell, and then Opie got to come live here with us."

"I want to live here!" shouted a little boy.

Lady chose that moment to lie down on the dirt floor and roll back and forth, her legs flailing in all directions. The children dissolved into laughter. Several boys began wiggling their arms in the air, imitating Lady's movements. Finishing her impromptu dust bath, Lady stood and shook from nose and tail, then joined Opie near the middle of the arena. Jodi invited two children at a time into the fenced area of the arena to brush the horses and spend a few minutes with them. The children eagerly lined up and tried hard to be patient. The third duo to join Jodi inside the arena rattled off a laundry list of questions while they brushed Opie and Bubba Jack.

"Do the horses know their names?"

"Is Bubba Jack one name or a first and middle name?"

"Do horses like pizza?"

"Do horses ever feel sad?"

Jodi noticed how the little boy's eyes searched Opie's as he asked that last question.

"They sure do. In fact, horses can feel all sorts of things. They can feel happy, sad, and even lonely." She paused for a moment, then turned to the rest of the children who were waiting with Amanda along the fence line. "What are some other feelings people have that you think horses might have too?"

"Silly?" a little girl shouted out.

"Maybe jealous? Like if their friend gets an apple and they don't?" another girl offered.

"I'd be mad!" a boy answered.

"Can they feel embarrassed?" asked another.

"People sure can have a lot of feelings, can't we?" Jodi said. "And you know what? Horses can too. For example, you saw Bubba Jack and Lady act a little silly, didn't you?" The children nodded and giggled. A few even brayed and wiggled, imitating the horses.

"I've seen Opie act a little lonely when the others don't let him eat with them. And I've seen some of our horses act mad and jealous. Of course, there's one feeling we haven't talked about yet that horses often feel. Can you guess what feeling that is? Do any of you ever feel scared or afraid?"

Every head bobbed in unison, and a few children shared specifics.

"I'm afraid of shots!"

"I'm afraid of the dark."

"I'm afraid of broccoli!"

"I'm scared I'm gonna die like Haley did."

Jodi couldn't tell who had spoken last, but the words brought a hush over the arena. It seemed to Jodi as if even the horses grew still, responding to the children's emotions. Jodi had often heard that a horse knows how you're feeling before you do, and in her experience, she had found it to be true. With their remarkable ability to sense and react to the slightest movements, as well as their ability to detect a human heartbeat from several feet away, it was no wonder horses could often deduce more from humans than humans could observe in each other.

"We sure know a lot about being afraid, don't we? Thank

you for telling me some of the things that scare you. You know what? I'm afraid of most of those things too."

"You are?" a few children responded in bewilderment. "But you're a grown-up!"

"I *am* a grown-up, but grown-ups get scared just like kids. And so do horses." Jodi nodded toward the back of the arena. "Do you want to know something that made Lady very scared a few days ago?"

Heads nodded in eager anticipation.

"A plastic grocery bag!" Jodi answered.

"A plastic bag?" the broccoli-phobic boy asked skeptically.

"It's true," Jodi assured him. "A plastic bag blew into the field, and Lady jumped up in the air, let out a loud whinny, and took off running as fast as she could to get away from it."

Some of the children laughed, but one little girl looked at Jodi, her face serious, and asked, "Why was she afraid of the bag?"

Jodi waited for the rest of the children to quiet down. "Lady isn't used to seeing plastic bags, and she didn't know what it was. You know, sometimes the things that scare us most are things we don't understand." Jodi paused for a moment to allow the children to process her words.

"But horses are big, and plastic bags can't hurt them," one boy said matter-of-factly.

"That's true. But they don't always know that. Horses have an instinct—a knowledge they are born with—which causes them to run away from anything that might hurt them. And since horses don't have claws or pointy teeth to protect them-selves, their instinct tells them to run away when they see some-thing that might be dangerous, especially something they've never seen before. Their instincts also cause them to stay in groups called herds because being in a group helps them stay safe. They can take turns watching for danger."

As if they had rehearsed this moment, Bubba Jack, Lady, Samson, and Opie stood together in the middle of the arena.

Jodi directed the children to Lady and asked, "Does Lady look scared right now?"

"No," the children chorused.

"Lady knows this arena, she knows me, and now she knows you. And she has her horse buddies with her. Lady doesn't feel afraid because she trusts us to take care of her, and she trusts her buddies to stay with her. It's almost like she's sharing her fears with them. Do you think it's good to share your fears with people you trust?"

Several children nodded.

"It is very good to tell someone you trust when you're feeling afraid. Or when you don't understand something. Or when something makes you sad or mad or happy," Jodi replied. "When we talk about our feelings—like what scares us—with people we trust, they can help us feel better and not be so scared."

"How would they do that?" the girl with wavy brown hair asked.

"Maybe they have been through something similar in the past, and they can tell you that it's going to be okay. Or maybe they can show you that the thing you're scared of is like a plastic bag and it isn't really as scary as you think it is. Or maybe they will tell you that it's okay to be afraid because it *is* a scary situation, but they promise to stay with you so you won't feel alone." Jodi pointed to the herd huddling in the arena. "Just like our horses are showing us now."

Several of the children stared in the horses' direction as Jodi concluded her impromptu speech. "I'm so glad you have people you can trust—people like Mrs. Jefferis, your parents, and the people who take care of you—and now me and my friends at HopeWell, and our horses." Jodi leaned forward and lowered her voice as if preparing to tell them a big secret. "Horses are great to talk to and share your feelings with because they know how it feels to be scared. And—" she paused for dramatic effect—"they are really good at keeping secrets!"

Several girls giggled.

"It's true. My horses have never told any of my secrets," Jodi said, with a smile. An alarm on her phone signaled it was time to transition the children to the next station.

"We have about ten minutes before Ms. Amanda is going to take you to meet our bunnies and see some more of the farm. If you would like to see the horses again, please line up here," she said, motioning to the gate. "And if you would like to write a note, or draw a picture for one of our horses, for Haley, or for anybody else, we have lots of paper, markers, and crayons on the table. And envelopes for you to put your notes in."

Ten minutes later, Jodi waved goodbye to the first group and hello to the next. The second group had lots to tell her about the bunnies, the goats, and the horses they had seen in the big field. She loved the energy they brought into the arena. And so did Bubba Jack. Within moments of their arrival, he let out another ear-piercing bray, clearly wanting to contribute to the conversation!

The second group's meet-and-greet went much the same as the first. Jodi was grateful to be able to talk in a non-threatening way about big concepts like fear and loneliness as they interacted with the horses. When their time came to an end, Jodi combined the two groups into one and led everyone out to the pavilion. She took time to answer questions about the animals until the children's parents and caregivers arrived. Amid goodbyes and thank-yous, Jodi felt a tug on her coat. Shontell's brown eyes were looking up at her.

"Can I see the new horse?"

It took Jodi a moment to understand what Shontell was asking.

"That's right! You were here the day we brought Solomon home, weren't you?"

"Yes. Why wasn't he here tonight?" she asked.

"He's still getting used to HopeWell and to his new friends. And we didn't want to scare him by bringing him somewhere he's never been before."

"Does he like it here?" Shontell asked.

Jodi wanted so badly to say yes. To tell Shontell that he loved it here, that he was loved by his new friends, and that everything was going to be great from here on out. But she couldn't lie.

"I hope he does," Jodi said honestly. "He's having a little bit of a hard time with his new friends. They aren't so sure about him yet. Actually, I think they are a little scared of him and they haven't been treating him very nicely."

"That happens sometimes," Shontell said with an authority that could only come from personal experience. "Can we go see him?" she asked again.

Jodi hesitated. Solomon hadn't been around children since his arrival just over two weeks ago. But she didn't want to disappoint Shontell either.

"I'll tell you what," she said, putting her hand on Shontell's shoulder. "If your foster mom says yes, we can go over to Solomon's field. We can't go in the field, but if he wants to come over to the fence, then you can say hi. We'll leave it up to him. How does that sound?"

Shontell's head bobbed up and down. "Great!"

Shontell's guardian gave her permission, and Jodi led the way to the pasture. Jodi stopped by the outbuilding that housed the switch to the electric fence so she could turn it off. Normally, it was left on 24-7 to prevent the curious and determined herd from breaking free and going on a joyride of the ranch. But Opie, Bubba Jack, Lady, and Samson were still in the arena, and Victory and the others were focused on the evening hay that had just been delivered. As they approached the pasture, Solomon raised his head and flared his nostrils, his ears tall and forward.

"Hi, Solomon!" Shontell called out. "Wanna come say hi to me?"

How could anyone not? Jodi wondered, compassion for this little girl flooding her heart. But Solomon didn't move. The rest of the herd looked in their direction, but when they realized Jodi didn't have any treats for them, they returned to their hay. Jodi was just about to explain that Solomon needed a little more time to adjust when suddenly he began walking toward them. Jodi had to fight hard to keep her mouth from dropping open in surprise.

"He's coming!" Shontell squealed.

Pure joy radiated from the girl's face. With all she had endured in her young life, it felt miraculous that something as simple as an approaching horse could bring such joy.

"Wow . . ." Shontell breathed the word, taking a step back

as she took in the large copper-colored horse standing on the other side of the gate. "He's really big."

Horse and girl stood facing each other for several moments. Jodi kept an eye on the rest of the herd, but they were so engrossed in their hay that they didn't seem the least bit interested in the meet-and-greet happening at the gate.

"Ms. Jodi?" Jodi's attention came back to the scene in front of her. "I like the white line on Solomon's face. It looks like someone drew on him with chalk. Can I touch it?"

Jodi didn't want to push Solomon or do anything that might add fuel to the simmering embers of herd dynamics. While Jodi worked hard to train their horses to accept human touches—especially being scratched, stroked, or petted—Jodi hadn't spent enough time with Solomon to know what he would tolerate. Better to play it safe. Jodi crouched down to talk to Shontell.

"I think maybe we should just say hi to Solomon with our words today. But maybe next time you come, you can touch the white stripe on his muzzle, okay?"

"Okay," Shontell agreed.

Jodi could sense the girl's disappointment, but Shontell simply raised her hand to wave at Solomon. Jodi watched in awe as he stretched his neck over the gate, lowered his head, and placed his muzzle at her eye level. Shontell froze. She shot a questioning look toward Jodi while Solomon stood perfectly still—ears forward, lips relaxed, feet still. Shontell's eyes were almost as round as Solomon's as she continued to stare at Jodi in an unspoken request for permission. Jodi nodded and mouthed *okay*. Shontell's face lit up as she slowly raised her right index finger and gently traced the white line from between Solomon's eyes to his nose.

"Hi, Solomon. I'm Shontell. I'm eight," she whispered, lowering her hand. "We both have S names."

Solomon bobbed his head twice and then pulled it back over the fence.

"Thank you, Ms. Jodi!" Shontell beamed. She looked behind Jodi and spotted her foster mom. "I think I have to go. Bye, Solomon! I'm glad you're my friend now."

Jodi was speechless as she waved to Shontell.

Well, I'll be . . . That was a coincidence, right? Solomon couldn't have known what Shontell wanted him to do . . . could he? She studied Solomon as he stood by the gate.

"You just made that little girl's day. You probably just made her whole week. What a gift you gave her." Jodi extended her hand to the horse and gently ran her right index finger down the white stripe on Solomon's muzzle. "Thank you."

"What's going on over here?" Linda asked curiously.

"I don't think you would believe me if I told you," Jodi said, still transfixed by Solomon.

"Try me."

When Jodi finished recounting the story, Linda's eyes twinkled in the way they often did when she had an idea she wanted to try.

"I'm afraid to ask what you're thinking, Linda."

Linda chuckled. "I'm just thinking it's time you start training Solomon on what it means to be a HopeWell horse," she said matter-of-factly.

"But he's still adjusting to the herd," Jodi protested. "I'm not sure he's ready."

Linda smiled. "I think he just told you he's ready. *And* we have a precious young boy who needs to meet him."

"You mean Shawn?" Jodi asked, picturing the twelve-year-old they had been unsuccessful in pairing with a horse. "But none of our current *trained* horses seem comfortable with Shawn's unpredictable behavior. How is Solomon going to be able to work with him?"

"Call it a hunch, but I think it's worth a try. And Shawn needs something bigger than the bunnies he's been working with."

Jodi looked from Linda to Solomon to the place Shontell had been standing less than ten minutes earlier. She remembered how gently Solomon had lowered his head to the girl. And how he had seemed to know what she wanted. As a cold gust of wind stung Jodi's face, the warmth of a promise fluttered through her heart. A promise God had given her that he would bring life from death, hope from pain, and light from darkness.

She wasn't sure how training Solomon fit into that promise, but she was ready and willing to try.

6

"COME ON, SOLLY. Don't walk away," Jodi pleaded with the horse, using her nickname for him. "I just want to take you to the hitching post." She pointed to the post less than fifteen feet away.

"Okay," she conceded, holding up the halter and lead rope she had been trying to hide behind her back. "Here they are . . . see? There's nothing at all to be afraid of. This is your ticket to having some fun outside the field."

Solomon stopped retreating. He looked at Jodi, then at the items in her hand. And took three steps back.

Ugh. Jodi checked her watch. She still had two hours before she needed to get cleaned up to take Jessica Christmas shopping. Jodi had been delighted when Jessica had sought out her opinion on a gift for Richard. And she had been overjoyed when

Jessica had suggested a Christmas shopping date. Granted, it had hurt a little when Jessica made her mom pinky-promise that she wouldn't be late or cancel at the last minute. Considering both of these things happened with more frequency than they should, Jodi had gladly linked her pinky with her daughter's. Jodi's willingness to make such a binding promise earned her a beaming smile from Jessica. It was a promise Jodi didn't think she would have any trouble keeping when she first entered the field more than forty-five minutes ago to collect Solomon for his first official training session. However, the two had been playing catch-me-if-you-can from the moment she had walked through the gate.

"Stay," Jodi commanded, as if talking to their dog, Traverse. "There is nothing to be afraid of. Come on, help a mom out."

Solomon looked from Jodi to his pasture-mates. He stomped his front hoof twice, walked toward Bubba Jack, and then lowered his head to the hay.

"I take it that's a no . . . ," Jodi mumbled.

Though it had taken many weeks and had its share of trials, the herd was finally taking to Solomon and allowing him in the group. Jodi was thrilled that things were peaceful now, but she felt an urgency to begin working with Solomon. She was confident he would be a quick learner. With two weeks to go before Christmas, if they started training now, he would have several months to get ready for therapy sessions before they started back up in April.

Jodi hated that they had to close sessions for the winter season. In an ideal world, HopeWell would be able to offer year-round sessions. But Michigan winters and an ideal world did not often go together. She was just grateful the bitterly cold weather had held off long enough for them to host their annual Christmas Open House for their current clients and volunteers. The November event—the last big gathering of the year—was always bittersweet. Jodi would miss seeing their clients, many of whom she had begun to think of as family. She worried about those facing difficult financial situations and wondered how they would fare during the harsh winter. She also worried about those struggling with deep emotional pain, those who were grieving, those who were lonely and isolated. Sometimes the gifts of empathy and mercy felt more like a curse than a blessing.

Jodi forced her thoughts back to the present. Other than praying for their clients and checking in via phone calls and emails, there was nothing she could do for them at the moment. *Actually . . . there is something I can do. I can train Solomon so that when our clients return, they will have another horse to work with.*

With renewed resolve, Jodi slowly approached Solomon.

"I know you can do this," she urged. Solomon turned and trotted to Victory.

"Great," Jodi sighed. "*Now* you're best friends. Remember, he's the same guy who chased you for *three straight days!*" Her voice rose on the last three words, causing several heads to turn in her direction.

While Jodi was venting her frustration, Bubba Jack approached and lowered his head for her. Jodi laughed.

"See, Solomon!" Jodi called out. "Bubba Jack loves the halter. He *loves* getting to go with me."

Since Bubba Jack was willing to have an adventure, Jodi placed the halter around his head and took hold of the lead line. As if she were Ree Drummond telling viewers how to prepare a feast for a hungry cowboy, Jodi narrated her every move for Solomon.

"First we place this lovely—and very soft—blue halter around your head. The color will look so beautiful against your chestnut coat. Once the halter is secure, I'll clip this lead line to it, and we'll walk together to the gate. Then I'll open the gate, and we'll head to the hitching post right over there."

After she had finished haltering Bubba Jack, she looked toward Solomon—hoping to find him so impressed with her thoughtful step-by-step instruction that he was standing behind Bubba Jack eagerly awaiting his turn. But . . . he was standing at the far end of the field with his backside toward her.

Perfect.

Bubba Jack swished his tail and pointed his ears toward the gate. He was ready to go.

Jodi checked her watch again. Two-thirty. An idea began to form—maybe if I take Bubba Jack for a quick walk to the hitching post and back, Solomon will get inspired and want to go for a walk too!

"Let's go, Bubba Jack," she said, with a flick of the lead rope.

Needing no further encouragement, the fuzzy donkey lifted his head and tail and headed straight for the gate. Jodi chuckled as he pranced his way through the exit.

Jodi followed Bubba Jack to the hitching post where the little donkey knew the routine like the back of his hoof: The hitching post is where adoring fans brush and groom you. Then you accompany your human companion on a walk—or if the human is small enough, you take them for a ride. Then you return to your field where you will be rewarded with a well-deserved treat.

When Bubba Jack arrived at the hitching post, he looked from left to right, twice.

"It's just me today, Bubba. But I can give you a good back scratch before taking you back to the field."

Bubba Jack lowered his head, and Jodi scratched his back, along his neck, and his backside too. That seemed to appease Bubba. As she led him back to the field, she noticed Solomon watching her.

"Ready to give it a try?"

Solomon didn't walk away.

Progress? Jodi dared to hope. She slipped the halter off Bubba Jack.

"Thanks for your help today."

Jodi checked her watch for the third time. *Forty-five minutes till I absolutely have to leave. That should give me time for one more try with Solomon.* She slowly approached him.

"Hey, Solomon," she spoke softly, "do you want to check out the nice halter Bubba Jack was just wearing?"

Solomon raised his head and flicked his tail. When she got within five feet, he turned and walked away. Jodi was determined to win this time. She had to. If she gave up now, all she would have taught him was that moving away from her was an effective way to get out of doing something he didn't want to do. She would not let his fear triumph.

Jodi approached him again. Solomon eyed her suspiciously while he took several steps in the opposite direction.

As Jodi mirrored Solomon's movements across the field in a slow waltz-like manner, a few of the other horses came to investigate. But when they realized Jodi didn't have any treats for them, they wandered away. Jodi's leg muscles began to burn as she continued to follow Solomon around the field. Thankfully, he grew weary before she did and stopped near the water trough. This time he didn't move when Jodi approached, getting near enough to stroke his neck.

"Good boy, Solomon," she soothed. "I know it's scary, but look how brave you are." She slowly raised the halter up to his head. "Now, let's just get this on, take a quick walk to the hitching post, and come right back. Then I can go . . ."

Solomon bolted. He was halfway across the field before he stopped.

Jodi looked at her watch to see how much time she had left. *Four o'clock!* She had lost all track of time while dancing with Solomon. She had no choice. She would have to start from scratch tomorrow. And this time she would block off the entire day.

"I'm here!" Jodi shouted, bounding through the back door. She had sprinted from the field to the house in less than five minutes and was trying to catch her breath.

"Jess?" she called, closing the door behind her.

Jessica walked into the kitchen. "You're here!" she said, unable to mask the surprise in her voice. She eyed Jodi's clothes and boots. Her left eyebrow rose slightly. "Are we still going shopping?"

"Absolutely! Just give me ten minutes to change."

Jodi kicked off her boots, ditched the shower idea, did a quick wardrobe change, and was back in the kitchen five minutes later.

"Wow! That was fast," Jessica said, a faint smile almost visible.

No medal or prize could ever compete with that smile.

The shopping trip was a success. Both of them found what they were looking for on sale. Jessica got the video game she had wanted for Richard, and Jodi bought new paint pens and plain ornaments to personalize. She had started doing that years ago for the kids, and it had morphed into a small business. But once she started HopeWell, the ranch demanded all of her time and attention. After picking up a few additional Christmas gifts, the two of them stopped for dinner at Culver's. As they were enjoying their milkshakes, Jessica surprised Jodi by asking about Solomon again.

"Well, actually, he was the reason I was a few minutes late," Jodi confessed, before telling her daughter of her failed training attempt.

"I'm sure he'll get it," Jessica assured her. "He probably just needs a little more time."

Jodi reached out and gave her daughter's hand a squeeze. "Thank you for saying that. I forget sometimes that not everyone moves at the same pace I do. I'm glad you reminded me."

For the moment, the distance between them disappeared. Jodi realized how much she had missed these little moments with her daughter.

"Now, enough about me and the ranch. I want to hear what's going on with you, Jess."

Jessica gave Jodi quick critiques about various books she had read, boys she thought were cute, and dreams she had for the future. Then her voice became quieter.

"Mom, I'm worried about my friend Christy," she confided. "I think she might have an eating disorder. And I don't know what to do."

Jodi had always been honest about her same struggle as a

teen and was grateful that Jessica felt safe enough to ask her for advice.

"Christy doesn't really have anyone to talk to about stuff like this," Jessica said. Jodi knew Christy's parents were embroiled in a nasty divorce, and Christy was caught in the middle. "I told her that she could always talk to you, Mom, because you understand how hard it is to be a teenager, and you never get all judgy and stuff."

"I would be honored to talk to Christy or any of your friends anytime, Jess. And I'm always here to listen to anything you have to say to me too." The seriousness of the moment quickly dissolved into laughter when an Oreo chunk from Jodi's milkshake got caught in her straw and she made a face like a fish as she tried to suck it free. They walked out of the restaurant together giggling.

On the way back to the van, they passed a man in the parking lot holding a sign that read "Hungry veteran. Please help if you can." Jodi and Jessica looked at each other, smiled, and walked back into the restaurant to get a gift card. Jodi handed it to the man and said, "God bless you for your service." The man nodded thanks, then hurried inside. During the drive home, mother and daughter sang Christmas songs at the top of their lungs. By the time Jodi pulled into their driveway, they were laughing so hard their stomachs hurt.

Following Jessica into the house, Jodi felt lighter than she had in years. She was hopeful that this was the beginning of a new chapter, not just for her and Jessica, but for their entire family. *Maybe I'm finally figuring out this whole working-mother thing.*

The smell of smoke from the kitchen redirected them. Jodi and Jessica were greeted by an agitated Ty.

"I'm not sure dinner is edible," he said. "And I'm pretty sure the oven needs to be cleaned."

Jodi didn't know if she should laugh, cry, or offer to help. Before she could decide, a wave of guilt hit her. She had forgotten to tell him she and Jessica were going out for dinner. *And . . . I should have offered to bring something for Ty and Richard*, she thought—belatedly.

"Um . . . Jessica and I actually ate already," Jodi admitted.

"What!" Richard protested from the family room. "Why did *she* get to eat out and I didn't? That's not fair!"

"Your mother and sister have every right to eat dinner together," Ty interjected. "Even if it means they leave us to try to digest charcoaled chicken bits."

Jodi appreciated Ty's understanding as she attempted to salvage some of the overly blackened meat, but it was a lost cause. Ty and Richard ate cereal for dinner.

As Jodi and Ty were settling into bed later that night, Richard poked his head in the doorway. "Can I go shopping with you tomorrow, Mom?"

Jodi stared in disbelief at her teenage son. *Why would he suddenly want to do that instead of spending time with his friends? Of course. Culver's!*

"Sorry, I have to work with Solomon tomorrow."

"That's not fair. Why can't I go? Jessica always gets her way."

"Richard, I have to work with Solomon tomorrow, but I can take you the next day."

"Could we get Culver's for dinner?" Richard asked before Jodi had finished speaking.

The laugh she had been holding back finally broke free. "Of course."

"Great! Goodnight!"

"Well, that was easy." Jodi laughed again.

Ty was scowling.

"What's the matter?"

"I'm really upset, Jodi."

Jodi mentally reviewed the entire day. *Had she forgotten to do something? Had she said something wrong? Was it an anniversary of some kind?*

"What's going on?"

"Everybody else is getting Culver's except me!" he teased.

Jodi playfully hit him with a pillow.

"How about Sunday? I might have to get a part-time job at Culver's to afford these special dates," she said, as she turned off the light.

Ty had been laughing, but he suddenly grew quiet. "Well . . . when you said 'part-time job,' it reminded me. I was paying bills tonight and looking over our accounts."

Jodi's stomach dropped. They had had enough of these conversations over the years for her to know what was coming.

"How bad is it?"

"It's tight," Ty said. "Not terrible, but with Christmas right around the corner, we're going to have to be careful."

He tried to inject levity into his tone, but Jodi could sense the weight he was carrying. She hated that she wasn't able to contribute to their income. She didn't draw a salary, and it took all the money they could raise just to pay for feed, veterinary care, and the day-to-day expenses of the ranch. Ty was carrying the financial burden himself. She was so grateful that he had a good dependable job, plus taking on odd jobs from time to time. And she was *so* thankful he was able to work as the facilities manager at HopeWell. But she felt guilty.

"We've managed tight before, and we will do it again," she tried to reassure him.

Ty leaned over and kissed her. "I love you."

"I love you too. And I have faith that everything will be taken care of."

And she did. However, she also made a mental note to count the number of ornaments she had purchased earlier. It might be time to resurrect the personalized ornament and art business.

7

JODI AWOKE THE NEXT MORNING with an unsettled spirit, but she couldn't figure out why. The sky was bright, her evening with Jessica had gone wonderfully, and while money was tight, it was nothing she and Ty couldn't handle. *Why do I feel this way?* She went through the motions of her morning chores, mumbling half-hearted prayers as she fed the animals. Jodi was so distracted in the tack room that she grabbed a training stick instead of the halter and lead line she needed.

After going back to get the right items, she paused before entering the gate. *What is wrong with me? Jess and I finally connected—really connected. That's what I've been praying about for years! So why do I feel so defeated? So irritable and restless?* Jodi shook her head in a futile attempt to clear it. She squeezed her eyes closed, curled her hands into fists, tensed the muscles in her legs, and began to count to ten, then allowed each muscle group to relax. She repeated the exercise two more times. The restless feeling didn't completely go away, but at least she felt calm enough to face Solomon and show him the halter was nothing to fear.

He didn't believe her.

Or, Jodi thought with an exhausted chuckle, *maybe he feels like dancing a jive today instead of a waltz.*

She tried her best to casually keep pace with Solomon as he darted around his pasture-mates, stopped for a few minutes to graze, then trotted across the field, before restarting his routine. Since her goal was to endure longer than his fear—not to cause more of it—Jodi didn't chase Solomon, or even walk directly toward him. But half an hour after first entering the field, she was panting—and seriously rethinking her career choice. As she paused at the water trough to catch her breath, she noticed Solomon watching. He was standing beside Victory, about fifteen feet from her.

"Go ahead and have your moment with Victory," Jodi called out. "But just know, I will win this time," she said, rubbing out a cramp in her side.

This training time needed to end on a positive note. After spending several minutes with her eyes closed and slowing her breathing, Jodi straightened up and opened her eyes. "Oh!" she gasped.

Solomon was standing less than five feet in front of her.

"Well, hi," she said softly. "You sure know how to surprise a person."

Jodi took two steps forward, mentally preparing herself for Solomon's retreat. But he didn't move. She took two more steps.

She extended the hand holding his halter. He didn't move. She stood on Solomon's left side and gently eased the nose band of the halter up his muzzle, brought the band behind his ears—the poll—then put the pull strap through the loop and secured it. Solomon was calm through the entire process.

"What in the world?" Jodi asked with a mix of frustration and amusement. "What was yesterday about? And all the fuss this morning? Did you just want to make sure I got my cardio in for the day?"

She attached the lead rope to the halter and held it in her right hand as she proceeded to walk toward the gate. Solomon walked right beside her. Bubba Jack met them at the gate.

"Sorry, Bubba Jack, not today."

Jodi had to push on the donkey's chest to get him to move out of the way. After a few moments, he reluctantly obliged. Once out of the field, Solomon began inspecting the patchy winter grass on the other side of the fence. It might not have been greener, but he still seemed quite intrigued. Jodi knew she could end their training here. He had done it. He had accepted the halter and been led from the field. But, in spite of her impromptu morning workout, she was still feeling restless and not quite ready to go home. And in a sign of faith—or maybe stubborn determination—she had set the grooming bucket out hoping she would be able to spend a few minutes grooming Solomon.

"Come on, big guy," she said, gently tugging Solomon's lead line forward. "Let's get you tied up to the hitching post over there and do a little grooming. Those dreadlocks in your mane could use a little attention."

Jodi was hopeful that working the tangles from his mane

and tail would work the unpleasant feelings out of her heart and mind. But Solomon halted his forward motion as they neared the post. Jodi applied pressure to the lead line and urged him forward. The horse jerked his head up and down in rapid succession.

"You're okay," Jodi soothed. "We're just going to stand next to that post, tie your rope to it, and then get you all gussied up for your friends."

Solomon's tail flicked several times before he began to move forward.

"Good boy, Solly. That's all you have to do—just keep moving forward."

As Jodi and Solomon came within a few feet of the post, she heard two quick beeps of a car's horn. Ty extended his arm through the window and gave her a wave as he drove by. She said a quick prayer for his protection as he drove his route. She then looked toward the house and wondered if Jessica and Richard were done with their morning schoolwork. From there, Jodi's thoughts began to snowball into wonders and worries. Jodi let out a deep sigh and was startled when Solomon did the same. His nostrils brushed against her chin.

"Sorry, bud, I forgot you were here."

Jodi squared her shoulders. The waitlist for HopeWell therapeutic services was growing by the day, so she needed to get Solomon client-ready.

Solomon's eyes grew wide and his nostrils flared as Jodi tied a quick-release knot through the O-ring on the hitching post. She left about two feet of slack in the lead rope—enough for him to move his head, but not enough to get tangled under his feet. As she began to brush his back, Jodi's thoughts returned to the waitlist of clients. When HopeWell had started, Jodi had wondered if they would have any clients. Now she feared having too many. As she moved the brush down Solomon's shoulder, she remembered the stack of messages Amanda had handed her yesterday from people inquiring about spring sessions.

"So many people need help . . . ," she whispered to Solomon.

As if materializing from Jodi's thoughts, Amanda called out from the office.

"Wow! I was just thinking about you," Jodi said.

"Good things, I hope," said Amanda.

"Always good things—except when you hand me stacks of messages," Jodi teased. She didn't want to burden Amanda, or any of the HopeWell volunteers, with her worries or concerns. It wasn't their job to comfort or reassure her. She was the leader. Ultimately, the buck stopped with her.

"So," continued Jodi, "what brings you over to the HopeWell horse salon?"

"I came in early to finish up some paperwork and get the last of the decorations put away from HopeWell's Christmas Open House. I just wanted to come say bye before heading out."

"Amanda, thank you so much for all of your help. You make all of this," Jodi swept her arm from left to right, "so much easier—and more fun. But I'm also glad you're taking a few weeks off to be with your family."

"Do you need any help before I go?"

"Actually, I left the detangling spray in the tack room. Would you mind standing with Solomon for a minute while I get it? He's been doing great today—well, relatively great," she clarified. "But I don't want to leave him alone tied to the post—and

I need a specific type of spray, but of course, I can't remember exactly where I put it."

"No problem. I'm happy to horse-sit for a minute."

Jodi hurried to the tack room, but she fumbled with the door latch for several minutes. As she stepped over the threshold, she tripped over the bucket full of brushes she had left sitting out. She quickly tossed them in the bucket and tucked it out of the way. After finding the detangling spray on a back shelf, she turned and bumped into a stack of rakes—sending them falling like a row of dominos.

"Great. Just great," she moaned. Jodi knew it wasn't a big deal, but she fought to hold back tears. After restacking the rakes, she made a quick exit before anything else could go wrong.

What is wrong with me today?

As she headed back toward the hitching post, she realized she had lost her motivation to groom Solomon. *I'll just get that large tangle out of his mane and then put him back in the field. Then maybe I'll lie down for half an hour to help me shake this feeling of . . .*

"Jodi!" Amanda screamed. "Help!"

Solomon was running frantically around the hitching post, his lead line wrapping tighter around it with each turn. *Oh no! What spooked him?* Jodi moved purposefully, lowering her voice, and talking softly and calmly to the big horse.

"Whoa, buddy . . . whoa, whoa."

Unfortunately, Solomon's fear instinct urged him to run harder and faster away from the perceived threat. His hooves were digging up chunks of earth around the post. This was the exact scenario Jodi would describe when teaching the HopeWell volunteers how to tie a quick-release knot at a hitching post. If a lead line gets wrapped too tightly around a post, a horse can actually pull the wooden post out of the ground—a frightening and dangerous scenario. Realizing the line was wrapped too tightly, Jodi attempted to untie the lead line from the halter. When that didn't work, she reached for the knot on his halter. With a flip of her wrist, she freed Solomon.

He ran ten feet toward the field and stopped, then lowered his head to the grass. Jodi and Amanda leaned against each other, exhausted from the ordeal.

"I am so sorry," Amanda said. "I got out my phone to take a picture of him and dropped it. It must have startled him. He tried to rear up and then started running."

Jodi put her arm around her friend. "He's fine. And this was not your fault, Amanda. I shouldn't have pushed him so hard on his first real day of training."

"Hey," Amanda countered, "if I'm not allowed to blame myself, then you aren't either."

Jodi attempted an appreciative smile. "I should have realized he wasn't ready for the hitching post today. I assumed he had done this with his other owners, but now I'm thinking he hasn't. Poor guy."

Jodi couldn't believe she had missed the signs of Solomon's stress. She wanted to berate herself for her mistake, for being so distracted. But she needed to check on Solomon and get him back to the safety of his field. And she needed to let Amanda be on her way.

"You have a vacation waiting. Solomon and I are fine. And you are exceptional. So get out of here."

Amanda searched Jodi's face. "Are you sure? I can help you get him back in the field."

"I am positive. He will be more than happy to get back to his hay. And I will feel much better knowing I'm not keeping you from your Christmas vacation. Amanda, sometimes I feel like you're HopeWell's own guardian angel."

Amanda laughed. "Oh, trust me, I'm no angel! But if you happen to have a solid gold halo lying around here, I'll gladly take it!"

After they wished each other a blessed Christmas, Jodi went to check on Solomon. He was ripping at every blade of grass he could find.

"You certainly earned some stress-eating time, buddy."

She didn't even attempt to put his halter back on. Not yet. She would give him a few minutes to eat in peace. Jodi turned her face toward the sun and closed her eyes for a moment of peace too. But that peace quickly evaporated as she thought about how badly things could have gone with Solomon.

Will he ever trust me again? For reasons she couldn't understand, she needed Solomon to trust her. Losing his trust was simply not an option. The stakes were too high. And with no one else available to train him over the winter, and finances too tight to allow them to keep a horse who couldn't work with clients, Jodi knew she had to do whatever it took to regain the horse's faith in her. Jodi took one last cleansing breath and slowly approached him.

"I am so sorry, Solomon. But you're safe now. And I won't let that happen to you again."

She felt confident she could keep that promise since she was already planning to cross-tie him for the foreseeable future.

Securing him with two lead lines tied to posts on opposite sides would mean he could only move front to back. No more running in fear circles.

Solomon glanced toward Jodi. Several blades of grass stuck out from between his teeth as he continued chewing. Jodi found the grinding sound his teeth made oddly comforting.

"There you go. You just keep eating that yummy grass while I put the halter back on you."

Solomon's eyes widened and his muscles tensed, so Jodi stopped moving. The last thing she needed was for Solomon to run off outside his field. She wasn't ready for another cardio workout this morning. Sad and frustrated, Jodi sank to the cold ground. *What was I thinking? What made me think training him today was a good idea? How am I going to convince Solomon to ever leave his field again?* And then, out of nowhere, Solomon's nose bumped her forehead. Jodi suppressed a startled cry. She had not expected to find him so close.

"Hi there," she said softly.

Jodi tentatively moved her hand toward his chin. When he didn't move, she gently stroked the side of his muzzle. When he still didn't move, she stood up and rubbed his neck. Realizing they weren't that far from the pasture gate, Jodi decided to try a new strategy. She took five steps toward the gate and stopped. Within two minutes, Solomon's nose bumped into her back. She took ten more steps toward the field and stopped again. A minute later Jodi felt Solomon's nose bump her shoulder.

"That's it. We'll do this one step at a time."

Jodi stopped about ten feet from the gate. Solomon halted and rested his chin on her shoulder. A single tear trailed down her cheek.

"I'm so sorry I was too distracted to notice your fear about the post. I feel afraid a lot too. And most of the time I'm not even sure what I'm afraid of." She turned toward Solomon. His whiskers tickled her cheek. "I'm so afraid of doing something wrong, of failing, of letting people down. But mostly I'm afraid of . . . It doesn't matter. You're safe. You're home. And all is well. That's all that matters right now."

Yet as she spoke the words, the unsettled feelings returned. Jodi opened the gate and walked inside, knowing Solomon would follow. A part of her wanted to stay with him, to linger in the field—to hide out for the rest of the day. But responsibilities called.

8

"Mom, it's freezing!" Jessica yelled from the pavilion. "What are you doing out here?"

Jodi closed her left hand around the hand warmer in her glove and continued patting Solomon, who was wearing a wrap blanket. "Just hanging with Solomon for a few minutes."

Christmas was five days away, and even though Jodi still had a stack of gifts to wrap, cookies to decorate, and a gingerbread house to construct with her kids, she had decided to sneak away after lunch to spend a few minutes with Solomon. It was something she had started doing every day since his panic-run around the post. At first, it was to make sure he didn't develop a fear of the hitching post, but after the third day she realized there was more to it than simply desensitizing Solomon.

After confessing her fears to him, she had started sharing

other feelings and thoughts too. And as she did, she noticed she experienced something with Solomon that she didn't experience with any of the other horses. A lightness perhaps? A quieting of her mind? Like an invisible weight was lifted from her shoulders every time she talked to him. She hadn't felt anything like it since high school, when her parents first enrolled her in the 4-H equestrian program.

Solomon was different from the rest of the herd, and Jodi realized their connection was unique. In fact, that connection caused her to forgo the formal training plan she usually followed, opting to spend time simply observing the horse instead. She wanted to learn Solomon's language, to allow him to set the pace, and to earn his trust. And as she did, she talked to him about everything.

Solomon bumped her shoulder with his chin, bringing her back to the present.

"I'll only be a few more minutes, Jess," Jodi said, leading Solomon toward the pavilion. "We'll still have plenty of time to build the gingerbread house before we have to get ready for tonight."

She and Ty and the kids were planning to drive to Loafers Glory in Blanchard to see the live nativity—the annual highlight of their family's Christmas season. The "village of yesteryear" with its shop and restaurant was always a favorite destination, but there was something sacred about it at Christmas. The area between two of the buildings was transformed to look like a road Mary and Joseph may have traveled in Bethlehem. Roman guards were stationed throughout the area, shepherds tended to their sheep in nearby pens, and, in what was always a moving moment, Joseph would lead Mary on a real donkey through the crowd and into a barn. After he shut the door, children dressed as angels would sing, and the entire area would be bathed in light. Every year Jodi would get goosebumps as a reverent silence fell over the crowd when Joseph opened the door of the barn, revealing Mary holding the infant Savior in her arms. The event always put the Christmas season in perspective for Jodi. And she suspected tonight would be no different.

"Hey, Mom!" Richard was running toward her. "Are we still doing the gingerbread house? I got all the pieces out."

"Did you eat any of the candies?" Jessica knew her brother too well.

"Um . . . only like two . . . or maybe five. No more than a handful."

"Richard! We need *all* of them to do it right!" Jessica protested.

"Ah, the joy of the Christmas season," Jodi said to Solomon. "See what you missed by not having kids."

While Richard entered the goat pen to visit Rosie, his favorite goat, Jessica walked over and patted Solomon.

"How's he doing?"

"He's good. Actually, he's really good," Jodi clarified, noticing Solomon's relaxed posture.

"So he's not scared of the post anymore?"

"No, thankfully, he doesn't seem afraid of it at all."

"That's good," Jess said. She looked at Jodi. "You seem different around Solomon."

"In what way?"

"I don't know exactly. I mean, in a good way. You just seem . . . I don't know . . . just like more yourself, maybe."

Jodi fought hard to keep her tears in check. She didn't want to scare Jessica with a big emotional display, but the fact that her daughter articulated what she had been feeling just moments ago left her a bit shaken.

Jodi touched Jess's arm. "Thank you for saying that. Solomon is a special horse. I think he's going to help a lot of people feel more like themselves. I'm just glad he gets to practice with me. But you know when I feel the absolute happiest?" Jodi asked.

Jessica shook her head.

"When I'm with you, your brother, and your dad."

Jodi knew her words had hit their mark when Jessica's cheeks flushed. And then the sweet moment was suddenly interrupted.

"Rosie! Get back here! That's *my* glove!"

Jodi, Jessica, and Solomon turned their heads simultaneously to witness the game of catch-me-if-you-can between Richard and Rosie. "Stop, Rosie! Heel! Halt! Mom, we need to teach the goats some commands!" Richard shouted.

"What do you think, Jess? Should we help?"

"Well, Richard *did* eat some of the candy without us, so . . . ," Jessica teased.

"Good point," Jodi agreed, then called out, "Run faster, Richard. You'll catch her."

"MOM!" Richard yelled in protest.

Jessica and Jodi walked together with Solomon to the field. Then the two of them joined in Rosie's game of keep-away until they finally intercepted her and returned the stolen glove to its rightful owner.

For the next two hours, Jodi worked on the gingerbread house with her kids—a house that would have been perfectly decorated, in her opinion, if there were just five more gumdrops on the roof.

9

JODI STOOD AT THE PASTURE GATE watching snow flurries land on Solomon's back. The tiny flakes lasted but a moment before being absorbed by his warm body. Normally, snow falling on Christmas Day would have had Jodi singing "White Christmas" at the top of her lungs. But the swirling white dust in the sky wasn't bringing her joy this Christmas. Instead, it simply felt like one more blow of disappointment.

Jodi pulled the collar of her heavy coat higher on her neck. She hadn't planned on visiting the horses this afternoon, not with hours of cooking still to do before her parents arrived for Christmas dinner. But of course, she hadn't intended on having an emotional breakdown while peeling potatoes either.

This Christmas Day had started like every other—full of laughter and joy from two excited kids. Jessica and Richard had bunked together in Jessica's room for Christmas Eve. It was a special tradition for the two of them, a chance to stay up late playing games and discussing what they might find under the tree in the morning. Jodi loved how close her children were. And she prayed they always would be.

Around seven that morning, she and Ty were awakened by giggling, followed by loud shushing. After hearing what sounded like buffalo running up and down the stairs, their official Christmas wakeup call commenced with an exuberant rendition of "We Wish You a Merry Christmas" before their bedroom door was flung open. Jessica and Richard each had a glass of orange juice in one hand and their Christmas stocking in the other.

Jodi loved this tradition most of all. No matter how old her children were each year, on Christmas morning they were still her little ones. Childhood wonder was still evident in their sleepy eyes. Jodi and Ty gladly accepted the orange juice, then watched as the contents of two stockings were poured out on their bed. Pencils, erasers, candy, playing cards, and other small trinkets were scattered like confetti on the quilt.

After the stockings were refilled with the bounty, the family headed downstairs to open gifts. Jessica and Richard seemed delighted with the hand-painted ornaments Jodi had made for them—a tiny rendering of the Titanic for Jess and a portrait of Rosie for Richard. Jodi had also loved the look of surprise on Ty's face when he unwrapped his gift.

"How in the world did you . . . ," he had mumbled, holding up the drill he had looked at months earlier.

Jodi smiled coyly. "I have my ways."

"Well, if they involve robbing a bank, I don't want to know," Ty joked.

"No bank robbing, I promise. Just some painted ornament sales," she confessed.

"You are amazing," he whispered. "Thank you for this."

Once all the gifts were opened, they piled in the minivan—the kids still in the pajamas Ty's mom had sewn for them—and made the short drive to Jodi's parents' house for more gifts and breakfast. Even though Christmas mornings were packed with activities and energy, they always felt sacred and peaceful to Jodi. Perhaps that was why it had caught her completely by surprise, after returning home from breakfast with her parents, when a familiar sadness fell over her. She fought hard to push the feeling aside, focusing instead on putting her gifts away and watching the kids enjoy theirs.

Just then Jessica ran into the family room wearing a new dress she had received from Jodi's mother. *She looks so grown up.* Gone was the little girl from this morning. In her place stood a beautiful young woman, soon to launch into her own life.

The realization hit Jodi with the force of a tidal wave. She loved that her daughter was becoming such a strong and capable woman, yet she ached for the little girl she used to be—the chubby-cheeked cherub who would run into her arms to show her something interesting she had found; who would reach for Jodi's hand when she was scared; and who twirled and sang when something touched her little heart. Parenting was an experience of grief and joy swirled together in the same moment.

"You look so beautiful, Jessica," Jodi said with a forced smile. "I, um, need to head to the kitchen and start prepping for dinner." Truthfully, her parents wouldn't be arriving for several hours, but Jodi hoped peeling potatoes would provide a much-needed distraction to curb her emotions. She smiled as she passed Ty and Richard locked in an intense game of checkers.

The moment Jodi was out of their sight, she allowed a stream of silent tears to fall. She quickly wiped them away with a Christmas dish towel and got to work. She peeled the first potato, placed it in a bowl of ice water, and then grabbed another. As she peeled, her thoughts drifted back to Jessica in her new dress. Suddenly, the image morphed into another dress. A much smaller dress on a perfectly formed newborn. Jodi's hand began to tremble, and the potato fell hard into the bowl, causing ice water to splash all over the countertop.

I can't breathe. She struggled to get air, her breaths coming in shallow pants. Her hands tingled, and her throat tightened. The room started to spin. She pulled her coat from the hook and rushed out the back door. She forced the cold air into her lungs.

Why today? she lamented. *Why does this have to happen on Christmas? I have to get my emotions under control. I don't want to ruin this special day.*

Jodi tried to pray as she walked toward the field, but no words came. Only memories. Memories she had fought hard to bury. Fought to keep locked away under a mound of business, positive thoughts, and willpower. But like a violent earthquake finding hidden fault lines and severing the ground beneath her, the memories now lay exposed. Refusing to be hidden any longer. As tiny snowflakes accumulated on the top of the fence posts, Jodi wrapped her arms around her abdomen. "Oh, Father," she cried, desperate for God to save her from tumbling into the pit she had worked so hard to climb out of—afraid that if she fell in again, she wouldn't have the strength to make it back out. And yet the moment the broken cry left her lips, her mind traveled back four years to a doctor's office when Jodi had uttered those same two words differently.

"Oh, Father!" Jodi spoke reverently as the doctor left the examination room so she could get dressed. Her hands tentatively touched her abdomen. "Pregnant? A baby? A baby! Thank you, Lord. What an unexpected gift."

At thirty-eight, with two soon-to-be teenagers, Jodi had been assuming that the lethargy, nausea, and general malaise she had been feeling the past few weeks was the flu. But following a negative flu test, her doctor had a hunch. The pregnancy test was positive. Today, the doctor performed an ultrasound to confirm the results.

"You are most definitely pregnant," the doctor said with a smile. "How are you feeling about that news?"

Jodi opened and closed her mouth several times before she was able to form any words.

"I . . . um . . . I think I'm in shock!" she said, as the reality hit her. "A baby! I'm going to have a baby."

As Jodi awaited the doctor's return, she wrapped her arms around her midsection, trying to cradle and protect the tiny life growing inside of her.

"Well, little one, you are certainly a surprise. Wait till your daddy hears about you."

Jodi called Ty from the parking lot to give him the life-changing news.

"Ty? Are you still there?" she asked when the line went silent. "Did you hear what I said?"

"A baby? Are you sure?" her normally unflappable husband choked out.

"I'm positive."

That evening the two of them sat at the kitchen table in silence for several minutes, trying to process that their family of four would soon become a family of five.

"I didn't know I wanted this, Ty. It wasn't even something I thought of, but now . . . I want this so badly I can hardly stand it."

Ty squeezed Jodi's hand. "Me too. We're having a baby!"

The next morning, Ty and Jodi gave Jessica and Richard the news. Initially, both of them were mortified, which made things awkward. But thankfully they started to embrace the idea of a new sibling. Jessica couldn't wait to hold her new brother or sister. And Richard was thrilled with the idea of not being the youngest anymore. Dinner conversations often centered around the tiniest member of their family. Would the baby have Jessica's eyes? Richard's dimple? Ty's chin? Jodi's nose?

Friends and family began dropping off baby clothes and equipment. Showers were planned. And Jodi's petite figure soon bore evidence of the baby growing inside her. Life had never felt fuller or richer. As Jodi cared for the children in the daycare she was running out of her home, she longed for the day she would get to care for her own baby.

That year, as an unusually harsh winter began to loosen its grip on central Michigan, Jodi began to feel run-down and more exhausted than usual. *It must be an early spring virus,* she thought. At twenty-one weeks, Jodi wanted to be on the safe side, so she scheduled an appointment in mid-May with her OB's office at the hospital.

As Jodi got ready, she made a mental list of the errands she needed to run after the appointment. *Pick up groceries, run by the post office, and possibly swing by the craft store to pick up yarn to start a blanket for the baby.*

But as she lay on the exam table, watching her doctor's face, she feared her errands would not get done.

After taking her vitals, the doctor said, "Your blood pressure is extremely high, and that concerns me. I'm ordering some additional tests." After several tests were done, Jodi's doctor ordered an IV and came in the room to explain what was happening.

"You have preeclampsia, a dangerous condition involving high blood pressure, swelling of the hands and feet, and possible kidney or liver damage. We need to admit you to the hospital immediately, in order to monitor this." The atmosphere in the room quickly became serious. Jodi made a brief phone call to Ty, unable to tell him anything other than "I have to go next door to the hospital." Ty must have left his mail route right away, because he arrived shortly after Jodi was wheeled into the obstetrics unit.

Jodi was in a quiet, darkened room and only allowed a few visitors—all in an attempt to keep her blood pressure from spiking any higher. She was given medication and put in pressurized stockings to force blood back to her heart. She also endured countless blood draws, until she felt like a human pincushion. But she didn't care. She would do whatever she had to do, wear whatever she had to wear, and brave an onslaught of needles if it meant her baby would be fine. But two weeks after being admitted to the hospital, obeying every order, following every recommendation, and praying countless prayers, a sonogram revealed what Jodi's heart refused to accept—her baby girl was gone.

A girl.

Her daughter. Gone before she could even draw a breath.

A sob ricocheted through Jodi's body as she stared at the monitor, holding tightly to Ty's hand.

"NO!" she cried, willing the monitor to beep.

Jodi couldn't reconcile the doctor's words or the eerily still picture on the sonogram with the vision she had seen of her future, of her family of five.

It couldn't be real.

And yet the next day when she delivered a perfectly formed little girl who had Jessica's eyes, Richard's dimple, Ty's chin, and Jodi's nose, she knew the future she had envisioned would always just be a beautiful dream.

Jodi held her tiny lifeless daughter and tried to say goodbye. But it all felt so wrong. They should be planning her coming-home party, not her funeral.

"She needs a name," Jodi said to Ty, her voice sounding far away—like it didn't belong to her.

He nodded, his eyes never leaving his daughter.

What do you name a baby who will never get to see the faces of those who love her? What do you name a child who will never hear your voice or feel your touch?

Jodi closed her eyes to ward off the pain. She cried out for mercy. She begged God for help, for a miracle.

As she lay with her daughter in her arms, she allowed herself to imagine a different reality, one only her heart could see. Her baby girl was smiling, wide-eyed and happy in the strong arms of Jesus. In that moment a sense of peace washed over her, allowing the vise grip of grief around her chest to loosen just enough for her to take a breath. And then another. As Jodi breathed in divine peace, she knew beyond a shadow of a doubt, that she would see her baby girl alive and well one day. It was a moment of hope that convinced her she would survive the pain, even as it threatened to crush her now.

"Hope," Jodi spoke aloud, forcing herself to look at her little girl.

"Hope," Ty choked out, rubbing the back of his finger across his daughter's beautiful little face.

"Mama loves you, Hope," Jodi whispered into her daughter's ear.

A blessed numbness started to wash over Jodi. Had the nurse put something in her IV? Or had her heart broken so much she could no longer feel anything? She didn't know or care. She succumbed to the numbness and fell asleep.

Two days later, Jodi left the hospital with empty arms and an empty womb.

The first day home, Jodi stayed in bed all day, too exhausted to move. But that evening when Jessica tentatively walked into Jodi and Ty's bedroom, her look of confusion, hurt, and sadness made Jodi sit up and open her arms to comfort her. Jessica had lost a sister. No words were exchanged between them. They just held each other until Jodi dozed off again.

The next day Jodi fought hard against the darkness that beckoned her to stay isolated, to stay numb. She could hear Jessica and Richard downstairs and knew they needed her. They needed to hear that everything was going to be okay, even if she didn't believe it ever would. She forced herself to get up and dressed and slowly made her way downstairs to join her family. Each action felt labored. Her limbs were heavy. Her mind was scattered. When she went to bed that night, more tired than she had ever felt before, she dreamed of Hope.

Her little girl was a toddler with chubby little legs that wobbled when she ran. The moment Hope spotted Jodi, she ran into her arms. Jodi swung her baby girl around and around, then kissed her before putting her down. Hope then turned and ran into the arms of the kindest-looking man Jodi had ever seen. He was smiling at both of them, and he lifted Hope high above his head, then settled her in his arms.

"Thank you," Jodi said to the man whom her heart instantly recognized.

"Daughter, your hope will rise again," he said, with a look so certain Jodi couldn't help but believe him.

Jodi nodded, blew a kiss to her daughter, and then woke up. The moment consciousness took hold of her, a wail erupted from her soul. It had felt so real. Oh, how she longed for it to be real. She wanted to go back to Hope, back to her dream. The weight of grief once again pressed heavy upon her, making it difficult to breathe. *No! I will not give in to the darkness. I will be strong for my family. I will be strong for Hope.*

Everyone was surprised when Jodi came into the kitchen.

"Hi, Mom!" Jessica and Richard said in unison, as Ty rushed over to pull a chair out for her.

Forcing a smile, Jodi said, "Good morning. How's breakfast?"

"Can I get you anything?" Ty asked. "Eggs, cereal, toast?"

Jodi wasn't hungry, but she knew she should eat something. Ty set a plate of scrambled eggs and toast in front of her. She forced herself to take several bites but soon felt nauseated. The kitchen was eerily quiet throughout breakfast. She wanted someone to talk, and yet she was grateful they didn't. She was touched by her family's concerned looks, but she was also desperate to escape. She remembered her doctor encouraging her to walk once she got home.

"Walking will help you build up your strength and stamina," she had told her.

At the time, Jodi had dismissed her doctor's instructions with a shrug. She didn't want to walk. She wanted to rock her baby. But now, a walk sounded like a good idea.

"I'll go with you," Ty said.

"Thanks, but I just need a moment alone. I promise not to go farther than the mailbox."

She could see the pain in his eyes as he held the door for her. He was trying so hard to hide it from her, but she knew. It was the same pain she had seen staring back at her in the mirror earlier that morning.

Jodi hadn't gone far before her tears began. They fell harder and more freely with each step. A few feet from the mailbox, she couldn't contain a wail that erupted from deep within. The cry was both frightening and cathartic.

"Why, God? Why didn't you save her?"

Jodi sank to her knees in the damp earth. Suddenly Ty's arms were wrapping tightly around her, his face pressing into her hair.

"I've got you," he whispered.

Ty supported Jodi as they walked back to the house. Jessica and Richard met them at the door with worried looks. Jodi knew they had witnessed her meltdown, and she hated to cause them more pain.

Over the next week, she started walking longer distances. She also started venting her questions, frustrations, and objections to God. After all, he said to cast all her cares upon him. And she believed that meant she could cast all her questions upon him too.

Why did you allow me to get pregnant, allow me to fall in love with a child, only to take that child away?

The God she prayed to, pleaded with, and believed in was as silent as the morning air. And yet, she still found comfort talking to him, peace as she cried out to him, and hope knowing that he heard her.

The unexpected hope Jodi found while walking around their property and talking to God each morning became a lifeline. It was just her and the God she knew was good, even when things felt so very, very bad.

Within a few weeks, Jodi's body grew stronger and her prayers began to shift from *why* questions to *what* questions.

"What would you have me do now, Lord?" she would whisper into the dark, after awaking from a nightmare.

"What is the point?" she would murmur in the predawn hours, after dreaming of Jessica and Richard playing with a healthy baby sister.

As her daily walks took her farther and farther into the untamed landscape of their property, Jodi began to wonder if they should clear out some of the overgrown vegetation. She had never given much thought to the seven acres they owned. It had always just seemed like a nice buffer from the rest of the world. After all, the half-acre surrounding the house was enough to maintain. Yet as she ventured farther each time, she felt more urgency about doing something with their unused land. When she mentioned it to Ty one night, he looked confused and uncertain, but he hadn't objected.

The next day Richard was up before Jodi. When she started lacing up her shoes, he asked if he could walk with her.

"I would love the company."

It was a quiet walk. Jodi could sense that conversation was far less important than spending time with her son. She led Richard to the section of land that had become a focus of her thoughts. As they approached the area, she watched his face closely. *Will he see something here? Will he see it as something more than it is?* His expression revealed nothing. Yet it was serene, lighter, and more at peace than she had recalled seeing him in a month. Whether or not Richard would share her vision or her drive to do something didn't matter. In this moment, he was at peace. What more could she desire for her son? For either of her children? Jodi hadn't realized she had stopped walking until Richard's voice broke through her thoughts.

"Mom, are you okay?" he asked.

"Oh, buddy. I'm fine," Jodi reassured him. "I was just thinking. I've been looking at this area the last couple of days, wondering if it would make a good field."

Richard's brow furrowed. "Why would we need a field?"

Jodi chuckled. She realized in that moment it was the first time she had laughed in the last month. It felt heavenly.

"I have no idea."

"Like, for animals?" Richard asked hopefully, raising his voice a full octave.

Jodi laughed again. She was glad her son had inherited her love of animals.

"Honestly, I don't know."

"Well, you should mark it off," he said decisively. "I think Dad has some stakes or posts in the shed. Want me to get them?"

"That would be great. Thank—"

Richard was off before Jodi got the last word out.

Within minutes, he dumped a wagon full of wooden fence posts and two shovels in a pile at Jodi's feet.

"Want me to help you?"

Jodi embraced her son, surprised to find that his shoulder touched her own. Within a month or two, he would be taller than her.

"Richard, thank you for being willing to help me. Why don't we put up one post, just to see if we can, okay?"

Mother and son worked together to loosen and move enough soil to create a deep hole. They centered the post inside the hole, refilled it, and tamped down the soil until the post stood firm. It was one lone post in the midst of an overgrown field. It served no purpose. Held no value. And yet, to Jodi, it represented something invaluable: enduring hope. Over the next week Jodi would walk to that post each day and ask God to bring purpose to her pain.

"Hope's life mattered," she declared to the trees one day during her prayer walk. "God, I don't know how, but please let Hope's life have meaning and purpose. I believe you can bring life where all I can see is death."

Jodi knelt in front of the post she and Richard had planted.

"Please, Jesus, bring life. Restore lives. Redeem pain and loss. I invite you here to this place. Whatever it is you want, I will do."

Jodi's heart felt a little lighter. She still grieved for her baby girl. She suspected she always would. But at that moment, her grief felt anchored to something. Anchored to someone. To Love and Hope himself.

Days later, Jodi spent the entire day putting up the rest of the posts.

Stakes of hope.

Stakes of promise.

Stakes that took on an entirely new purpose when Jodi read about a ministry in Oregon that paired hurting children with rescued horses in order to help both find healing and purpose. It was as if God had illuminated a neon sign that said, DO THIS. She had obeyed and started HopeWell Ranch, in memory and honor of her baby girl.

As the vivid memories of the death of Hope and the birth of HopeWell began to fade that Christmas morning, Jodi spotted Solomon in the pasture resting between Victory and Lady. Solomon had truly become part of the herd, even rising in the hierarchy. After the incident at the hitching post, it seemed Solomon had become a rock of stability, calm and steady. It was almost as if he had run all the fear out of himself that day and now nothing scared him.

Jodi remembered her promise to Solomon that he would never be lonely at HopeWell. She was grateful to have been able to keep that promise. "Do you ever miss the friends you had at Ken and Sue's?" she spoke into the wind.

She tried to imagine a younger version of Solomon standing in Ken and Sue's field between the two horses she had seen in the photos at their house.

"Of course you do," she decided for him. "They were a part

of your past, a part of your story—a part of you. How could you not miss them?"

A broken sob erupted from her lips at the last word. She shook her head against another tidal wave of emotions. She began to shiver—both inside and out.

"Oh, God," she cried out, startling the horses. "Why does it still hurt so much?"

Jodi sank to her knees and squeezed her eyes closed.

"She should be here . . . ," she mumbled, tasting the salt of her tears. "It's not fair! You should . . . Oh, my sweet baby girl, I am so sorry."

As the cold earth seeped into the knees of Jodi's jeans, a rush of air warmed her forehead. She opened her eyes and saw a familiar hoof on the other side of the gate.

She reached through the slats to touch Solomon's front leg. The horse didn't move. His quiet presence steadied her. It was time to pull herself together. Her parents would be arriving soon, and she wanted everything to be perfect for Christmas dinner.

"Kinda looks like someone wants you to let him in."

Jodi hadn't heard Ty arrive.

"Technically, I'm the one on the outside of the gate. He's already in."

"I don't think that's the case. I don't think he's really in at all," Ty said, kneeling down beside her, wiping a tear from her cheek. "But I know he sure would like to be." Ty's eyes pleaded with her. "Will you let him?"

"Oh, Ty. I miss Hope so much."

"I do, too, sweetheart," Ty said, enveloping Jodi in a hug. Several silent moments passed before Ty spoke again. "Why didn't you come get me? Or tell me how you were feeling?" he asked, pain and love evident in his voice.

"Because I didn't want to bring you and everyone else down. The last thing I want to do is ruin everyone's Christmas. I have so much to be thankful for. I should focus on that, right?" She could feel her cheeks flush. "I mean, no one wants to hear me talk about my dead baby at Christmastime."

Jodi flinched at her words. Ty did not.

"Jodi, look at me," Ty said, lifting her chin with his finger. "Hope will always be a part of our family. She will always be a part of us—a part we lost far too soon. She deserves to be talked about and remembered—especially at Christmas. I haven't brought her up because I didn't want to make you sad. I thought maybe you never talked about her because you had somehow found a way to move on, and I didn't want to ruin that for you." He tucked a wispy section of hair back under her hood. "But I can see now that was the furthest thing from the truth."

"Oh, Ty . . ." Jodi didn't know whether to laugh or cry.

She chose to laugh. But Ty's expression remained serious.

"The kids talk about her with me," he confessed.

"They do? They never talk to me about her."

"They don't want to make you sad."

Jodi shook her head. "We are quite the bunch, aren't we? I'm trying to protect you, they're trying to protect me, you're trying to protect all of us."

"No wonder I'm tired all the time," Ty teased, adding, "I'm also freezing."

Ty stood, brushed the dirt from his pants, and extended his hand to Jodi. He pulled her up and into his arms.

"Can we make a pact here and now to stop hiding our

feelings from each other? Please? I want to know what's going on with you, Jodi. All of it—the good, the bad, and everything in-between. Please let me in to that beautiful heart of yours. And I promise that I will try not to make everything a joke all the time. I think sometimes I do that to avoid the hard stuff, you know?"

All Jodi could do was nod. At that moment Solomon softly nickered. The sound startled both of them. Ty looked from the horse back to Jodi. His eyes narrowed as if he were attempting to solve a puzzle.

"Is that why you've been spending so much time out here? Do you come out here to talk to him?"

"Um . . . sometimes," Jodi confessed, shrugging apologetically.

"I don't know what it is about him," she continued, "but I feel lighter when I'm with him. Like somehow he really understands the loss I feel better than I do. Does that make any sense?"

Ty nodded, walked up to the gate, and stood in front of Solomon.

"Thank you," he said softly.

As Jodi walked back to the house hand in hand with Ty, she couldn't help but feel like she had just experienced her very own Christmas miracle.

Later that night as Jodi sat at the table surrounded by her family, and wrapped in memories and laughter, she felt something she hadn't felt in a very long time. Real peace. Once dessert was served, everyone made their way into the family room where the conversation continued.

"Hey, Mom, wanna take a selfie with us?" Jessica asked, holding up a paper Santa hat on a stick.

Jessica and Richard had received the photo booth prop set as a gift. They had created a backdrop from a white sheet and were filling everyone's phones with festive selfies. Watching her kids laugh and act like carefree teenagers was a balm to her soul.

"You bet I do!"

Jodi dug through the props. She held elf ears to her face for the first photo, reindeer ears to her head for the second, and a gingerbread-man mask over her face for the third.

"Mom, I can't see you through that mask," Richard said, laughing.

Jodi took one last picture in which she held both a Santa hat and a speech bubble that said Ho-Ho-Ho. But as she switched places with Ty, she found herself replaying Richard's words: *I can't see you through that mask.*

Is that what I've been doing, Lord? she wondered. *Am I wearing a mask to keep others from seeing the real me?* Jodi unconsciously touched her cheek. She had never set out to hide her feelings—or her heart—behind a mask. But as she reflected back over the past few years, she realized how often she had pushed her feelings aside in an attempt to protect someone else; or put on a happy face when all she wanted to do was cry; or pretended all was well when it was anything but. And so, with the people she loved most gathered around her, she silently let go of her mask, offering it to the One who had filled her heart with peace and freedom. It was far from a fair trade, but she was convinced it was a trade God delighted in making.

10

JODI SOAKED IN THE SUNSHINE. After two weeks of bitterly cold temperatures and on-and-off snow showers, an almost-sixty-degree day in early March felt downright tropical.

"Isn't this wonderful?" Jodi said, standing next to Amanda at the hitching post with Solomon.

"I can't believe it! I wonder how long it will stay like this?" Amanda responded. Jodi looked from the goats to the rabbits to the horses and found each group basking in the sun. Several of the horses were lying down—totally relaxed for the first time in fourteen days. Jodi hoped the next round of storms wouldn't be as severe as the one that had just come through.

"The forecast calls for another cold front later this week. So I guess we'd better enjoy this while it lasts."

As if agreeing with Jodi, Solomon extended his head toward her and exhaled what sounded a lot like a sigh of contentment.

"I couldn't agree more, Solomon." Jodi laughed, rubbing his neck.

"I still cannot believe how calm he is right now," Amanda said.

Jodi had forgotten that the last time Amanda had seen Solomon tied to a hitching post, he had been anything but relaxed. It had taken weeks of slow, purposeful work to desensitize and recondition him to accept the post. The first few times, Jodi simply walked him in a wide circle around the post, gave him a food reward, and then took him back to the pasture. When Solomon showed no fear of getting close to the post, Jodi had decided it was time to try cross-tying him to two hitching posts. She fed him apple slices while he stood between the two posts. After several days of him readily accepting the cross-ties, Jodi had moved to one post. The methodical and time-consuming process had paid off, and now Solomon was able to stand patiently at the post while Jodi groomed him.

Of course, the real test had come several weeks ago—just as the weather was turning stormy. While he was standing at the post for what Jodi assumed would be his last training session for a while, a dump truck went barreling down the road, its uneven load rumbling loudly. Solomon's ears had flown forward. His head popped up, and his muzzle tightened.

Jodi started speaking softly and calmly to him. "That noisy old truck is almost gone. You're safe." She tried to get him to focus on her. He had passed his final hitching post test with flying colors, and Jodi knew he would be ready when sessions started back next month.

"You worked hard to overcome your fear, didn't you, Solly?"

Jodi reached into her back pocket and pulled out an apple-and-oat-flavored treat. Solomon eagerly accepted her offering, then nosed her jacket for more. Jodi gave a gentle push to his chest to get him to take a step back.

"I really think he's going to be a great addition to sessions," Jodi told Amanda. "After all, he's had a lot of practice being my own personal therapy horse."

Amanda opened her mouth but then quickly closed it. Jodi could see that she wanted to ask a question. And as much as Jodi didn't want to answer, she knew she needed to do this. This would be *her* test—her own dump truck moment of sorts—to see if she could open up to Amanda. And it did feel like a test, especially since Amanda had recently been dealing with her own heartache: her daughter Harleigh had been diagnosed with a growth disorder. Jodi wanted to rise to the challenge. She had promised Ty—and God—that she would share her struggles with people she trusted and allow them in.

"While I've been working with Solomon," Jodi began, "I've started talking to him about some things that I've been feeling—things I haven't wanted to share with anyone else."

"Jodi, is everything okay? Are you okay?"

"Oh, I'm fine—really. I'm not sick or anything. It's nothing like that." She was quick to assure her friend. "I just realized that somewhere along the way I started keeping my feelings to myself. But over Christmas I had a bit of an epiphany. By trying to hold my grief and my fears to myself, I was trying to hold something that was too heavy for me to carry alone. Does that make sense?"

Amanda silently nodded.

"On Christmas Day, Ty found me crying by Solomon's field, and we had a long talk. Since then I've been trying to share more with him. And I've kept talking with Solomon. I mean, I've been talking *to* Solomon—he doesn't talk back or anything."

Amanda chuckled. "I know what you mean."

Jodi swallowed hard. She felt self-conscious about talking so much. She felt a gentle touch to her shoulder.

"Thank you for sharing this with me, Jodi. And for trusting me enough to do so."

A deep sense of relief washed over Jodi. She knew it would take a long time to undo some of the patterns she had set. But she had passed this test.

∪

"Good job, Solly!" Jodi praised Solomon when he halted beside her in the round pen.

Jodi was taking advantage of another break in the weather in order to get some extra training time in. Following the unexpected—and short-lived—early March warm front, they had experienced fifteen days where the high temperature barely made it past the freezing mark. When Jodi had stepped outside this morning to temperatures in the forties, she decided that after her prayer walk and feeding time, she would resume Solomon's training. With sessions starting in less than two weeks, she wanted to be sure the horse was ready.

They had spent the morning working on various ground-work exercises. Working with a horse from the ground—as opposed to sitting on his back—helps build trust with the horse and will usually make the transition to riding much easier. Jodi had begun their round pen time with leading exercises to ensure

Solomon was comfortable being led on a halter and lead line all around the enclosure. She alternated between leading Solomon from in front—called the lead position—and from the partner position, where she led from beside his shoulder. Both would be important skills when working with a human partner.

Jodi also spent time on touch exercises—getting Solomon used to receiving touches from human hands—of all sizes and experience levels. Since children made up the largest group of HopeWell's visitors, the horses needed to be prepared for excited, tentative, and even awkward touches.

This was a lesson Jodi put at the top of the training list after an awkward moment with one of the first visitors to HopeWell. One little girl got so excited to touch Opie's muzzle that she started bouncing up and down—and accidentally shoved her hand in the horse's nostril. Jodi had been both amused by Opie's dazed and confused look, and worried that the rough and un-expected touch would make him hesitant to be around other children. Thankfully, Opie took the unexpected nose incident in stride and continued to be a dependable, even-tempered horse in sessions. But the incident was an important reminder of the need for every HopeWell horse to be desensitized to touches, as well as to loud noises and unexpected movements. As prey animals whose instincts tell them anything and every-thing is a threat and could kill them, horses will run, kick, or freeze when frightened.

Solomon was no exception. Jodi picked up the training stick and touched Solomon's back, legs, undercarriage, and neck. Happy that he had handled the training stick so well, she repeated the exercise with her hands. She knew he would receive her touch well since she had been grooming him and spending so much time with him, but she was working hard to follow the normal training protocol so that Solomon received the same training as all the other horses.

Next, Jodi brought out some orange safety cones to see how he would handle a foreign object in his space. Jodi lined up the cones in the middle of the pen and allowed Solomon to set the pace on whether he would investigate or keep his distance. He eyed the cones suspiciously for several minutes. His ears twitched backward, then forward, and he stomped at the ground. After deciding the cones were not a threat, he lowered his head and took a few tentative steps forward. Jodi held the lead line loosely in her hand and walked with him. Solomon sniffed the first cone, mouthed the second, and turned over the third with his teeth. Jodi righted the cone and then led Solomon to one side of the round pen.

"Now, Solly," Jodi began, "we're going to walk beside the cones on one side and then come back on the other side."

Although most people might think it odd that she was explaining things to a horse, her overall philosophy was to think about what you are going to do; feel the motion of what you are going to do; then do it. When a horse is fully engaged and attuned to a trainer, the horse can sense what is expected of them—even before they are asked to do it.

Often when leading a horse in the pen or arena, Jodi would simply think about stopping, then feel what it's like to stop— and the horse would stop. It took a lot of time and effort to train a horse to anticipate a command, but with most of the healing work at HopeWell coming from the relationship that is formed between horse and human, Jodi knew that the hard work of training often leads to profound results.

Now, as she stood in the round pen, she looked toward the end of the line of cones. She imagined taking that first step with Solomon. She inhaled deeply and then stepped with her right foot. Solomon's legs moved a fraction of a second after hers. Jodi led him to the left of the cones. She had to gently pull on the lead line twice to bring his attention and focus back to her when he started to veer off course. On the return trip down the other side of the cones, she only had to bring his attention back once. As they approached the last cone, Jodi thought the word *stop*, pictured where she would stop, exhaled, and came to a stop—at the same time as Solomon.

"Good job. That's enough for today, Mr. Smarty-Pants. Let's get you back to your field for some well-earned hay."

Jodi rubbed Solomon's side, scratched his rump, planted a kiss on his nose, and then led him to the field. As she opened the gate, she saw Victory limping toward them. Several days ago, Jodi had noticed him favoring one of his back legs, but by the afternoon he had seemed fine. However, his ears were now pinned back, his muscles tight, and he was barely putting any weight on the other leg. Jodi slipped the halter off Solomon and attempted to get a better look at Victory's hoof. But Victory wouldn't have any of it. *Time to call Dr. Pol.*

11

"It's an abscess," confirmed Dr. Pol—Jodi's veterinarian for the past fifteen years—after examining Victory. "And a bad one at that. But we'll treat him, get him all fixed up, and this old boy will be good to go."

Jodi appreciated Dr. Jan Pol's matter-of-fact way of speaking and his take-charge approach to things. No matter what was going on with one of their animals, whether a life-threatening issue or a mild illness or injury, she always felt better the moment Dr. Pol or his veterinary partner, Dr. Brenda Grettenberger, pulled up the drive—even when a camera crew pulled in behind them.

When Jodi had called earlier in the day to make Victory's appointment, she had felt relieved—and then a little guilty over her sense of relief—when she learned there would be no filming today. *The Incredible Dr. Pol*, the popular reality show based on his veterinary practice, was on hiatus for the next few months. Since the show premiered in 2011—after his son, Charles Pol, pitched the idea to network executives—Jodi and a few of the HopeWell animals had been featured in several episodes. And with the way viewers were responding to the show, Jodi suspected they would be featured in many more episodes over the years. Jodi had grown to care as deeply for the film crew as she did for Dr. Pol; his wife, Diane; their son, Charles; and Dr. Brenda. Yet she always felt anxious when the cameras were rolling. She figured she must hide her nerves well though, since the executive producer often told her what a natural she was in front of the camera. Thankfully, she didn't have to worry about any of that right now.

Dr. Pol went right to work. He cleaned the well of Victory's hoof with a pick, getting out the tiny rocks and other debris that had gotten lodged in the crevices. He then used a hoof knife to cut away at the bottom of the hoof until he could reach the infection. After relieving the pressure, Dr. Pol applied copper sulfate and wrapped Victory's hoof in gauze and vet wrap.

"Keep it wrapped for a week," Dr. Pol instructed as he put his instruments away. He then handed Jodi a bottle of SMZ antibiotics. "He'll need twelve pills twice a day."

Jodi was well acquainted with the large amount of medications needed to keep thousand-pound animals healthy. Dr. Pol gave Victory a pat on his rump.

"Call me if things seem to get worse. Otherwise I'll be back out next week to check on him."

"That sounds good. Thank you so much, Dr. Pol."

Several hours later, as Jodi was attempting to hide a dozen

chopped-up pills among the grains in Victory's bowl, she studied the herd eagerly awaiting their evening meals. Victory stood in his normal position near the water trough, his back leg cocked slightly to keep pressure off his foot. But to Jodi's surprise, Solomon was standing next to him. She couldn't believe he could go from bottom to top in the herd in just six months.

After filling the rest of the horses' bowls and loading them in the wheelbarrow, she pushed it toward the nine hungry horses lined up at the fence. "Just call me president and chief operations officer of the HopeWell meals on wheels program." She laughed, then cringed when the wheels squeaked loudly. "Better make that the meals on *squeaky* wheels program."

∪

"Are you sure this is the same horse?" Linda called out as she observed Jodi and Solomon in the arena. "The one you were complaining about late last year because he was too distracted and stubborn to get any training done?"

"Yup, same horse!" Jodi answered.

"Wow," said Linda. "Apparently, he just needed a little time to adjust to his new home." Jodi handed Solomon a treat. He had just completed an obstacle course that required him to walk along a series of safety cones, maneuver around hula hoops, and then come to a stop between two plastic chairs. He had navigated the course flawlessly.

The real test had come a moment later when Linda stepped on a squeaky toy to see how Solomon would respond to an unexpected and strange noise. Other than a twitch of his ear in the direction of the sound, the horse had barely reacted. Linda's expression was a mix of delight and surprise. Jodi had a theory about Solomon's calmness at the noise. After all, the squeaky toy sounded a lot like the wheelbarrow she used to deliver their food! *Who knew that even a squeaky wheelbarrow could serve a purpose!*

After rewarding Solomon with a back scratch, Jodi led him through the course again while Linda used squeaky toys, maracas, and a whistle to make a variety of sounds. The added distractions required Solomon to focus more than he had the first time through the course. Jodi could tell by the way he moved his mouth that he was thinking hard and processing the sensory stimuli as he walked the course. Sometimes horses will even open their mouths comically, almost as if attempting to swallow new information. Solomon's tongue was working as hard as his brain and his feet as he navigated the course and kept his attention on Jodi. As the duo stopped between blue and red plastic chairs, Jodi gave Solomon a thorough scratch.

"You are going to help so many people out here—just like you've helped me."

"Jodi, what do you think caused his transformation?"

Jodi thought for a moment. "Well, I think it's like you said—he just needed more time."

Linda seemed to ponder Jodi's words. "Yes, I do think that's a part of it, but he seems so different now. He's relaxed, at ease, and displays a trust in you that he didn't before. I just wonder . . ." Her voice trailed off, but Jodi could tell by the way she studied Solomon that she was far from done with her analysis.

"You seem different too, Jodi. You seem more relaxed and at ease . . . more open, maybe? When exactly did Solomon start becoming the model of attention during training?"

"Let's see, back in December I started spending one-on-one

time with him. But because of the hitching post incident I told you about, I didn't ask much from him. I just wanted to build his trust in me and give him positive experiences near all the posts we have around the ranch."

As she reflected back to those days, a few memories surfaced. "I did try a few times back then to do some lead exercises, but he would either tune me out or try to drag me back to his field. It was like a switch would get flipped and he would just be done."

Lost in her thoughts, her hand rested on Solomon's back.

"Where did you go just now?" Linda asked, her voice filled with compassion.

"Sorry, I didn't mean to zone out. I was just thinking about Christmas Day."

Linda motioned toward the door, and the three of them headed silently toward the large field.

When they got to the gate, Jodi continued. "I had a kind of realization this past Christmas. Well, actually," she quickly clarified, "I had a breakdown that afternoon, which led to a realization later that evening."

Linda nodded, encouraging Jodi to keep talking.

"I think it just all hit me that day—Hope not being there and me not wanting to upset anyone by telling them how sad I was. Then there was the fact that my kids are growing up so fast. It was like sweet memories were bubbling to the surface, where they started mixing with the pain of memories we would never get to make. And somehow a day of peace and joy turned into an overwhelming feeling of loss and pain. Which then made me feel guilty because I really do have so much to be thankful for . . ." Jodi shrugged, unsure of how to end her impromptu confession.

"You said you had a breakdown," Linda prodded gently. "So I take it all those thoughts and feelings came out at some point that day?"

"Oh, they definitely came out. I didn't want to lose it in the house and upset everyone, so I took a walk. Eventually, I found my way to the field, my feelings found their way out, and . . ." Jodi paused. "And Solomon found me."

Jodi leaned toward the horse as she told Linda about her conversation with Ty, her commitment to share more of her heart, and her epiphany of wearing a mask in an attempt to protect others from her pain. Linda listened intently, and the two of them fell into a comfortable silence. Jodi opened the gate and led Solomon through. She removed his halter and left him to his herd.

"What happened to Victory's foot?" Linda asked, pointing to the wrap.

"Dr. Pol had to drain an abscess."

Jodi shared Dr. Pol's treatment plan and praised Victory for handling it so well.

"Why do you suppose you feel the need to hide your feelings behind a mask?"

The question startled Jodi. It took her a moment to transition from Victory's abscess to her emotions.

"Well, I guess because I don't want to be a burden to anyone—especially to those I love who are dealing with their own problems," Jodi answered, feeling more vulnerable than she had in weeks.

Linda's eyes were full of understanding, but there was also a hint of something else. "So it must be a pretty big burden for you to care for Victory then, huh? You must feel weighed down by having to tend to his wounds when you're already having to do so much around here?"

At first Jodi was slightly offended by Linda's questions. But when she saw the tenderness in Linda's eyes, she knew she had walked right into the wise woman's carefully constructed trap.

"I see what you're doing," Jodi said, grinning in amused defeat. "And no, of course I don't see caring for Victory as a burden. It's an honor to care for him, especially given how well he cares for so many who come through our gates. But that's different, and you know it," Jodi clarified. "I'm not having to bear Victory's physical pain, and I don't have an abscess of my own that I'm trying to deal with while caring for his."

Linda pushed back.

"No, I don't think the situations are that different at all, Jodi. Sure, one's an injury to a foot and one is a wound of the heart, but both cause pain, both require letting the toxins out in order for healing to begin, and both will heal much more quickly when trusted others help tend to the wounds. And," Linda said, moving to stand right in front of Jodi, "you yourself said it was an honor to care for Victory, a joy to walk alongside these horses and let them know they are not alone. By hiding your pain behind a mask, you are denying Ty, your kids, and those of us who love you, the honor and joy of walking with you through this, to remind you that you are not alone."

Jodi blinked hard and realized she was holding her breath. "Thank you, my friend," Jodi whispered.

"It *is* an honor to walk alongside you," Linda said, pulling Jodi in for a hug. "And while I imagine your instinct will always be to try and hide your pain from others, fight that instinct as hard as you can, okay? We want to walk with you. We want to help you carry this, Jodi."

Jodi could only nod. Thankfully, she didn't need to talk because Linda wasn't quite done.

"So you said that Solomon became more cooperative after Christmas?"

"Yes . . . ," Jodi answered, unsure of where this was going.

"You know what likely happened then, right?"

"Linda, I have absolutely no idea what you are talking about right now!"

"Once you allowed your mask to fall off, Solomon began trusting you to lead. After all, that's why horses make such great therapy partners—they don't see masks."

Of course! Jodi couldn't believe she hadn't put all of that together before now. Horses don't—and can't—see pretense; they can only see what is. If a human is feeling anger when working with a horse, the horse will sense that anger—even if the human is smiling or able to fool all the other humans. The horse will detect any emotion and mirror back those same feelings, by becoming distant, aloof, ornery, or uncooperative. A huge part of equine therapy is helping humans interpret a horse's demeanor and behavior, in order to help the person uncover their own feelings.

Solomon saw my true feelings, mirrored them back to me, and stayed with me through it all.

Jodi turned her attention back to Linda. "So you think that when my actions matched my feelings, Solomon finally felt like he could trust me to train him."

"Exactly. When he first arrived at HopeWell, he saw you as

a kindred spirit—a grieving, wounded spirit. But now, I think he sees you as a leader. An authentic, trustworthy person who knows that a good leader depends on her herd to help her lead."

Jodi watched Solomon nudge hay toward Victory as the two stood at the hay feeder. He was becoming a leader among his herd. And even more important, he was a horse who had completely stolen—and was helping to mend—her heart. Just like she anticipated he would help mend the hearts of many others, once sessions started back up in two weeks.

12

"YOU'RE MAKING ME DIZZY with all that pacing," Ty said, as he turned off the morning news. "I take it the phone call you just got wasn't good news?"

"Two miniature horses need a home."

"Really?" Ty asked excitedly. "Haven't you been talking about getting a miniature horse so little kids would have a horse more their size?"

Ty's eyes were open and searching, clearly trying to make sense of Jodi's hesitation.

"Yes . . . but . . ." Her words trailed off. She was unsure of how to explain the worry gripping her heart.

Ty placed his hands on Jodi's shoulders.

"I know you wish you could go out and talk to that horse of yours, but the thunderstorm outside isn't cooperating. I would be more than happy to listen to whatever's spinning through your mind. I mean, I'm no chestnut stud, but I'm still a pretty good listener."

"He's a gelding," came Jodi's automatic retort. Then she started laughing at her husband's favorite running horse joke. The momentary laughter broke her defensive wall, and she suddenly wanted to share her fear with Ty.

"Linda and I have been talking about how nice it would be to have a mini, but we were talking about someday in the future, not today. And we were talking about one mini, not two. *And* we were hoping for one that was trained and ready to start working with children immediately, not two that have been living in questionable conditions, locked up in a twelve-by-twelve dog kennel and have never interacted with children—or had positive interactions with any humans. And then there's the added cost. It surely can't cost that much to feed them, but there's farrier costs and vet costs, and someone will have to train them, and even then we don't know if they will be able to be used in sessions . . ."

Jodi paused to take a breath.

"Sorry, that was probably a lot to dump on you," she said sheepishly.

Ty pulled her into his arms. "Thank you."

Jodi squeezed him tight.

"So what are we going to do about these two minis?" asked Ty. "Yes, there are some obvious cons on the list, but are there any pros?"

"Well, we really could use some smaller horses. And even if they can't be used in sessions right away, kids could still look at them and we could talk about them—maybe incorporate them into the program in other ways." Jodi looked out the window toward the field.

"And we do have the smaller field already set up, so they could go in there, I guess. I have been praying recently about a mini, but I just assumed God's timing was a little further out, you know? I just don't know if this is the right time, or if these are the right horses." She rubbed her neck. "And I don't want to make a mistake."

Ty opened his mouth to say something but was interrupted by Richard.

"What mistake don't you want to make, Mom?"

"You made a mistake?" Jessica asked, following her brother into the family room.

"Good morning," Jodi greeted them. "There are muffins on the counter if you'd like those for breakfast."

Jodi turned back to Ty, anxious to hear what he was thinking. Jodi needed to make a decision one way or another. She wanted to give the woman plenty of time to find another home for the horses if HopeWell wasn't able to take them.

"What were you going to say, Ty?" she asked, before glancing back to see her children still standing in the middle of the family room.

"Don't you want breakfast?" she asked, trying to hide her annoyance.

A little line appeared between Jessica's eyebrows as she studied her mother. "What mistake are you worried about making, Mom?"

Jodi waved her hand as if shooing a pesky fly. "It's nothing, sweetheart. I was just talking to Dad about some HopeWell stuff. Nothing for you to worry about."

A shadow of disappointment fell over Jessica's face as she retreated to the kitchen. Richard silently followed behind. Ty nudged Jodi's knee and nodded in the kids' direction.

I did it again, Jodi realized with a pang of defeat. *The kids were showing real interest and genuine concern, and I blew them off.*

"Hey, guys," she said, following them into the kitchen. "I'm sorry. I didn't mean to make you feel excluded. I'm trying to make a decision about adding two more horses to the herd—two miniature horses," Jodi clarified.

"Why would that be a mistake?" Richard asked.

"Well, it will cost more money, for one thing," Jodi answered. She pulled out a chair at the table and motioned for the kids and Ty to join her. "And there would be two horses coming instead of one, which would mean double the money. And since they would be coming from a less-than-ideal situation, I'm not sure that we would even be able to use them in sessions. It's just a lot to consider."

The room grew quiet for a moment, and Jodi questioned whether she should have shared as much as she did. She didn't want Jessica and Richard to have another reason to feel resentful of HopeWell. They had just recently seemed more interested in the ranch—and more willing to help out from time to time. What if they started to resent how much of the family's money went to supporting HopeWell? Jodi shifted in her seat. *If only I could have walked this morning. No one else would have had to listen to my internal conflict—except maybe Solomon.*

"Mom?" Jessica's tentative voice interrupted Jodi's thoughts. "What situation are the horses coming from? You said it was less than ideal—in what way?"

The concern, evident on Jessica's face, warmed Jodi's heart.

"The horses have been living in a small dog kennel, and while it sounds like their owner thought she was taking care of them, the farrier says the two have been horribly neglected through ignorance."

"So the horses need someone who knows what they are doing to give them a safe home?" Jessica asked.

Jodi nodded, but before she could say anything, Richard added his opinion. "You know more about horses than anyone."

Jodi appreciated his words—and the sweet way her son was trying to encourage her.

"That's quite an exaggeration." Jodi laughed, handing him another napkin. "But thank you for saying that."

Jessica continued. "And Hopewell would be a safe place for them to live. We have tons of space and a good vet who can help them heal. And maybe the minis can help others who have been neglected like they have. That's kind of how HopeWell works, right?"

Jodi stared at her children. How long had she waited—prayed—for them to take an interest in the mission of HopeWell? And feared they never would.

"Well," Ty said, rising to his feet, "it sounds to me like your kids vote *yes* for the tiny horses. And they made such a good argument that I vote *yes* with them," he added, giving Jessica and Richard a wink.

Jodi looked at her family and their enthusiastic smiles. "You're sure?" she asked.

They all nodded their heads in unison.

"Well, if everyone is in favor of this, I have a phone call to make!" Jodi said, pushing her chair back.

Richard had gotten up to get a second muffin, but he quickly spun around. "Really?" he shouted. "We're getting two miniature horses? This is the best day ever!"

"Didn't you say that last month when we got a new goat?" Jessica teased.

After a quick phone call, Jodi, Ty, and the kids spent an hour making plans for the arrival of two miniature horses. Jodi was so delighted to be working with her family, she didn't even notice that the rain had stopped.

Everything was still drying out when Jodi walked into the arena several hours later. Linda was sitting at a picnic table, writing in her notebook.

"Sorry I'm late. I was on the phone making arrangements to bring two miniature horses here later this week."

After she filled Linda in on the few details she had about the minis, the two turned their attention to the upcoming session.

"Shawn will be here in about forty-five minutes. When do you want to go get Solomon?"

Since Shawn had difficulty coping with a lot of external stimuli, the women had decided to have the first meeting between him and Solomon take place in the arena. While most sessions involved going to the field to halter a horse and leading it to a hitching post or to the arena, Jodi and Linda felt strongly that the HopeWell program needed to fit the individual—and not the other way around. So when adjustments had to be made, they were happy and eager to make them.

"I'll go get Solly in a few minutes. I want him to have lots of time to adjust and settle in here before meeting Shawn."

Jodi's stomach clenched as a barrage of doubts flooded her

mind. *Was Solomon ready for this session?* Perceptive as always, Linda interrupted Jodi's mental tailspin.

"All we can do is try," she said. "You've done a remarkable job with Solomon. We've seen firsthand how sensitive he is toward others. And Shawn's mother is willing to give it a try. So . . ."

Jodi finished Linda's sentence. "That's exactly what we are going to do. And pray—a lot," she qualified with a wink.

Jodi and Linda were standing near the parking lot when a dark blue minivan pulled in. Shawn's mother, Mrs. Mitchell, stepped out first, waved to Jodi and Linda, and called out a cheerful hello. Moments later, the passenger side door opened, and Shawn slowly emerged. His gaze was focused on the ground as he and his mother approached Jodi and Linda.

"Hi, Shawn! Linda and I are so glad to see you today."

Shawn looked up for a moment. "Hi," he said, raising his forearm in a wave.

Mrs. Mitchell exuded joy. "We are having a very good day today," she said jubilantly, before lowering her voice a few decibels. "He's been pretty calm the past few days. I'm not sure if it's the new diet we're trying—no gluten, no sugar, no dyes—or just him feeling calmer than usual. But he seems happy. Right, buddy?" she asked, giving her son a thumbs-up.

Shawn stuck his thumb in the air. "Right, buddy," he said, his gaze still on the ground.

Thank you, Lord, Jodi silently praised as she turned to Shawn.

"Shawn, Linda and I have a special friend for you to meet today." Jodi pointed toward the arena. "He's in there waiting for you."

Shawn's gaze followed Jodi's hand, but then quickly fell to the ground again. Mrs. Mitchell gently placed a hand on her son's shoulder. "Meeting new friends is nice. Will you go with Jodi and Linda to meet your new friend?"

Shawn looked up at his mother and gave her a faint smile. She nodded reassuringly as the four of them began walking toward the arena. Once inside, Linda engaged Mrs. Mitchell in small talk, while Jodi and Shawn continued through the gate. Solomon was enjoying the freedom of being at liberty, without a confining lead rope. As Shawn intently watched Solomon sniff the arena floor, Jodi looked up at the clear panels crowning the arena. Sunlight was flooding in, and she could see dust particles dancing in golden streams through the sunbeams, transforming them into a thing of beauty. Jodi's attention returned to Solomon and Shawn. The two stood across the arena, silently studying each other. Finally giving in to his curiosity, Solomon began to move toward Shawn. Shawn cast a worried look at Jodi, searching for reassurance that the large animal meant him no harm.

Jodi walked over to Shawn and smiled. "It's okay, Shawn. This is Solomon. He just wants to come over and say hi."

As if sensing the boy's concern, Solomon stopped three feet away from the boy.

"Do you know how to do a cowboy handshake?" Jodi asked.

Shawn shook his head but never took his eyes off the horse.

"You bring your hand up like this," Jodi said, walking toward Solomon. She held her hand in a relaxed fist as she reached it up to Solomon's nose.

Solomon brought his muzzle to Jodi's hand and bumped it. The horse then let out a deep sigh. Sensing Solomon's gentleness, Shawn followed Jodi's lead and did the same. When Solomon bumped his nose on Shawn's hand, his face lit up. Feeling more confident, the boy reached out and gently stroked Solomon's cheek repeatedly. Jodi thought possibly that Shawn liked the feel of horsehair on his hand. Solomon stood quietly as Shawn patted his face, then his neck. Soon Solomon dropped his head and closed his eyes. *He's asleep!* Jodi marveled.

She watched as the same boy who at a previous session had screamed and cried and kicked, now stood with his forehead on Solomon's side. His head moved up and down with each breath Solomon took. It was like watching the personification of peace. Jodi knew she would never grow tired of seeing a horse and a human—especially a child—find understanding and comfort in each other.

Jodi glanced at her watch. *Where did the time go? Thirty minutes have passed, and it seems like Shawn just got here!* It always amazed her how quickly peaceful moments seemed to pass. Even though she hated to interrupt the beautiful scene, she knew she needed to get ready for the next session.

"Shawn," she whispered. Both horse and child looked at her. "Would you like to walk Solomon back to his field with me?"

Shawn nodded and looked Solomon in the eye. Solomon let out another deep sigh. Jodi got the lead rope and showed Shawn where to clip it onto Solomon's halter. Then she showed Shawn where to walk safely in relation to the big horse and allowed the boy to lead Solomon from the arena. The only sound Jodi heard was the clomp of Solomon's hooves, yet she had no doubt a deep communication was taking place between the boy and horse. It seemed as if the pair had formed a bond within the span of minutes, and they now moved in synchronized under-standing. Jodi believed Solomon had quickly understood that Shawn needed him to be calm and steady, just like he somehow sensed that Jodi had needed him to provide a listening ear while she talked and sorted through her feelings.

She stopped her musings as they arrived at the gate where Bubba Jack greeted them.

Jodi laughed. "We need to watch this one! He's an escape artist!"

Shawn never once looked at the donkey. His eyes were for Solomon only. Jodi went through the gate first and pushed the friendly donkey back so Shawn could bring Solomon into the pasture. A whinny greeted them from across the pasture.

"Lady is happy you are back," Jodi said to Solomon.

"That's his friend?" Shawn asked.

It was the first sentence Shawn had ever spoken to Jodi. She fought hard to calm the storm of emotions she was feeling.

"Yes, Lady is Solomon's friend. She's part of his herd—that's what a group of horse friends is called. They stay in herds because that helps them feel safe."

Jodi showed Shawn how to unhook Solomon's halter and carefully pull it over his ears. When Solomon rejoined the herd, Shawn continued to watch him.

Sensing an opportunity, Jodi asked, "Who are your friends, Shawn?"

"Solomon is my friend. Shawn is safe with him."

13

Four years passed. Jodi and Ty were glad to be inside this morning in a warm kitchen reading the newspaper and drinking coffee as the wind howled and icy sleet pelted the windows. The TV weatherman was predicting a long winter and had said the ice would quickly turn to snow. Jodi prayed he was right. Snow was one thing; ice was an entirely different beast. She was glad to have cleats to put on over her shoes when it was time to feed the horses later.

"Will I ever get used to how quiet the house is?" Jodi asked.

She took a sip of coffee, savoring the warmth. So much had changed over the past four years. HopeWell had added several more horses, rabbits, and goats, along with two dozen volunteers, three part-time staff, and four additional outbuildings to hold supplies and equipment. But the biggest changes had been on the home front.

Six months ago, Jessica had bounded up to Jodi while she was filling a water trough. "Mom! I got into the ministry studies program at church! I'll be starting classes in a month and will get to live in the parsonage. Isn't it great?" Of all the things Jodi had been expecting that day, her daughter's news was not one of them. Jodi knew Jess had a heart for missions and the church, but she wasn't prepared for things to change so quickly.

"That's wonderful, Jess," Jodi said, feigning excitement.

That night, Ty encouraged Jodi to focus more on the exciting new chapter Jessica was beginning than on the sweet chapter they were closing. She tried, but it was hard. Within a month they moved Jessica into the parsonage and she was thriving in the program. Not one to be left behind, Richard was spending a great deal of time either working or with friends. Jodi knew that within the next year she and Ty would officially be empty nesters.

She looked around the kitchen. "I can't believe how much I miss the noise and chaos. I mean, look at this place! It's almost too clean to feel like our house!"

"A quiet and clean house," Ty said. "It is a hard, hard burden to bear. I have the perfect solution. We could bring a few of the goats inside. Quiet, clean house problem solved."

"Ha!" Jodi laughed, nearly choking on her coffee. "That's *just* what we need. I guess if that's my alternative, I will take a quiet, clean house."

Jodi opened her mouth to say more, but the words stuck as she saw a headline in the newspaper and quickly scanned the story.

Clare County Animal Control seizes nine horses and fifty dogs from horrific conditions. Following a call by a concerned citizen, officers were dispatched to a local residence where they found animals kept without access to food or clean water and in small, confined spaces. Most of the animals are malnourished and suffering the effects of neglect. Many of the mares are pregnant. Unclear at this point if owner will be charged.

"Ty, did you read this?"

"Yeah, it's horrible."

"Those poor animals. How awful," Jodi murmured.

"I know what you're thinking," Ty said, without looking up from the sports page. "And I love you for it, but I don't think . . ."

"But Ty . . . they need somewhere to go, and we . . ." Jodi's face fell as the reality of their situation hit her. "We don't have the resources to take on any other horses right now, do we?"

Ty shook his head. Jodi knew he was right. Just the night before, she had been running the numbers. With the four horses they had added since Solomon's arrival, their veterinarian, farrier, and feed bills had gone up quite a bit. The hay they received last month would have to last them till spring. And with the weather as bad as it had been, Jodi couldn't imagine bringing malnourished and traumatized horses to the ranch. It wouldn't be fair to the horses, and it wouldn't be fair to the animals already in their care.

"I can't imagine what those poor animals have lived through. I just wish we could do something . . ."

"I know. But maybe it's someone else's turn to rescue these horses. Maybe someone else needs to experience the blessings that can come from stepping in to help."

Jodi knew he was right, but she still couldn't stop thinking about the abandoned animals.

"Jodi, look out there." Ty motioned to the pastures and fields. "Look at all that God has accomplished through you—through HopeWell—over the past eight years. Think about the horses you *have* rescued—including the two miniature stinkers who chewed up my gloves last week!" He furrowed his brow in pretend outrage. "Think about the hundreds—the thousands—of sessions that have happened out there. The wounds that have been healed, the lives that have been changed. Think about the camp we hosted last summer for the kids who have survived cancer. Do you remember the look on that little girl's face when she started singing while riding Solomon? Remember how her mom broke down in your arms because that was the first time she'd heard her daughter sing since her diagnosis?"

Jodi nodded, tears welling in her eyes.

"I love your instinct to rescue anything that breathes—heavens, that's probably why you married me! But please don't forget to celebrate what God has *already* rescued through you."

"Okay," Jodi mouthed, knowing once again that Ty was right.

For the rest of the week, as the unrelenting cold front continued to blanket HopeWell in snow, Jodi busied herself with a variety of home projects. She cleaned out and organized two closets, a bathroom vanity, and her dresser drawers. She made several batches of soup, countless loaves of bread, and several dozen cookies. But no matter how busy she stayed, she would still find herself worrying about the recently rescued horses. *Were they somewhere safe? Did they all survive? Would they ever fully heal?*

On Friday night, she walked into the family room as Ty was watching the local news. Images of malnourished horses filled the screen. Jodi sat down beside Ty and turned up the volume.

"We have an update on a story we first reported last week of Clare County Animal Control rescuing nine horses and fifty dogs from a local woman's property. A spokesperson from animal control tells us that they are working with nearby shelters to temporarily house and help rehome the dogs. We've also learned that a local couple has opened up their farm to all nine horses. 'We have the space,' they said when we reached out for comment, 'and they need a second chance.'"

"Oh, thank God they're safe," Jodi whispered.

"They are safe," Ty repeated. "Someone else stepped up and gave those horses a good home."

Jodi picked up the remote to turn off the television when a lead-in for the next story came on. After the commercial break they were going to report on the plight of homeless veterans in need of shelter during the bitter cold that was gripping central Michigan.

"Oh God," she prayed aloud, "please provide rescue for these veterans just like you did for the horses. Please wrap these brave men and women in your arms and send them someone to show them what your love looks and feels like."

Trying her best to leave the veterans and horses in God's hands, she walked into the kitchen to start dinner.

14

JODI LIFTED HER FACE to the April sun. The warmth felt so good after months of a bitterly cold winter. She walked through the gate to the large field, with a handful of freshly pulled spring grass hidden behind her back.

"Solly!"

Solomon's ears flicked a moment before he started moving toward her. The day was bright and clear, but recent rains had left the pasture a muddy mess. Jodi stood on the dry patch of ground near the gate. She had enough to do today without having to add boot washing to the list.

"Well, hi," she said, opening her hand to the horse.

Solomon used his upper lip like a spoon to scoop the spring grass into his mouth. As he chewed his gratitude, Jodi ran her hand under his mane.

"Oh, Solly," she exclaimed, as her fingers got caught in a

mud-encrusted tangle, "you are a mess. That must have been quite the mud bath."

A quick look at the rest of the herd revealed Solomon was not the only horse who had enjoyed the cool mud.

"Thankfully, we have a bunch of kids coming for sessions, and they will get all of you cleaned up." Jodi picked up another section of his mane caked in dry mud. "Did you roll in *every* mud puddle you could find?"

Solomon bumped Jodi's leg with his nose.

"I take that as a yes," Jodi said, laughing.

It felt good to stand in the field with Solomon again. Other than quick visits during feedings, Jodi hadn't spent much time with the horse in several months. Last year, when Jessica was making plans to move out, Jodi had spent many hours with him. Yet the more time she spent sharing her heart with Solomon, the more distance she felt between her and Ty. She didn't want to wake up one day and find that the two of them had drifted apart, so Jodi decided to talk to Ty about her feelings instead. It hadn't been easy. But knowing the stakes were high, Jodi persisted.

At first, it felt awkward and clumsy. She never seemed to say what she meant, and most of the time she didn't even know what she meant or how she felt. She would become flustered when Ty would ask clarifying questions. They seemed like accusations, even though he assured her they weren't. A simple question like "Why do you feel that way?" sounded like "You shouldn't feel that way" to her. It took a lot of practice, several arguments, and a willingness on Jodi's part to take Ty at his word and a willingness on Ty's part to give her time to talk through and sort out her feelings before asking too many questions. But eventually they were able to talk freely about everything from mundane moments to future dreams to feelings, fears, and triumphs.

Now, as Jodi stood facing the mud-splotched horse, a wave of gratitude washed over her.

"Thank you for helping me through some of my darkest and hardest days, Solly. We've come a long way, haven't we, buddy? Sometimes I feel like you were sent here just for me. Like I was your own special project." Jodi shook her head in wonder. "You have helped so many people out here, haven't you?"

As Jodi kissed a clean part of Solomon's cheek, she noticed a little drainage from his nose. She stepped back to take a closer look at him. His nostrils were slightly flared. Jodi listened carefully. His breathing did sound a little labored—nothing terrible. But since he had been diagnosed with asthma three years earlier, Jodi had learned the importance of being proactive when it came to Solomon's symptoms—which always seemed to get worse in the spring and fall. She hoped there was something they could do to keep that from happening this year.

As soon as she returned to the HopeWell office, she called Doctor Pol's office. Doctor Brenda said she would come by the next day to check on Solomon. After making note of the appointment time, Jodi turned on her computer and opened her email inbox. Thirty minutes, and a dozen emails later, her cell phone rang.

"Hi, Jodi. It's Kathy. How are you?"

Jodi was always glad to hear from her friend at the Department of Health and Human Services. "I'm doing really well. It's so nice to hear from you."

"Well, I'm glad you are feeling that way because I'm actually calling to ask a favor."

"Ask away."

Assuming the favor had to do with a referral or with someone Kathy wanted to bring out for services, Jodi was surprised at Kathy's next words.

"Could I give your phone number to a couple who has been fostering nine rescued horses?"

Jodi sank down in her chair.

"I heard about that horrible situation months back. Ty had to talk me out of trying to bring all the horses here. I wanted to help so badly, but I knew we couldn't provide what they needed."

"You might still be able to help. It turns out the couple—Denny and Gail Sprague—was hoping to talk to you."

"Those names sound familiar," Jodi said, interrupting Kathy. "But I can't think of why . . ."

Kathy was able to solve the mystery.

"Gail is actually a good friend of mine. She said that you got some hay from them several years ago."

"Oh my goodness. That's right!" Jodi exclaimed. "We had just started HopeWell and were still learning how much hay it takes to feed a herd. We'd been told about some people selling hay at a good price, and that's when we met Denny and Gail!" Jodi smiled at the memory. "They were so kind. It took us two trips to haul all the hay back to the ranch. And they wouldn't take any money for it. They wanted to support HopeWell with that generous gift.

"Yes, please give them my number," Jodi said, suddenly remembering Kathy's question. "I would love to talk to them. In fact, I'd love to return the favor and send them some hay, if they need it."

Jodi heard Kathy chuckle softly. "Well . . . one of the horses they rescued could certainly use some hay, as well as a place to live."

Kathy quickly continued, "Seven of the horses have already been rehomed. And Denny and Gail decided to keep the oldest mare." Kathy started talking so quickly that Jodi had to listen closely to keep up. "Turns out that all but one of the mares was pregnant. They were all in a small enclosure with a stallion. Oh, Jodi, it was so bad. The poor things had no food or fresh water. They were surviving on tree bark and their own fecal matter. They were so traumatized that they couldn't even be trailered for transport to Denny and Gail's."

"What did they do?" Jodi asked, feeling nauseous.

"Well, since Gail and Denny don't live that far from where the horses were found, Gail came up with the idea to walk them to their property."

"Denny and Gail walked nine horses to their property? In the dead of winter?" Jodi marveled.

"Yep, Gail, Denny, and a small army of volunteers walked the horses half a mile—through the snow and wind—to their new temporary home. It must have been quite a sight."

"A horse parade," Jodi said, picturing the scene in her mind. A parade of rescue. *Of freedom.*

"It sounded pretty incredible," Kathy said. "Well, Gail called me yesterday because they have one last horse in need of a home. She's a sweet pony mare, around two or three years old. Gail says she follows Denny around like a puppy dog. Miraculously, she was not pregnant. Gail thinks the mare could be a good fit for HopeWell."

"I'll need to talk to Ty and the team here at HopeWell before making any decisions," Jodi said.

"I understand, Jodi. Thanks for even being willing to talk with Gail. I'll send her your number and let you amazing ladies take it from there."

After the call ended, Jodi sat in her chair for several minutes trying to wrap her mind around it all. "Lord, I never imagined that the people we have been praying for since January were people we knew—people who supported HopeWell at the very beginning! But you knew . . . you knew." Jodi pressed her back against the cushion and rubbed a knot in her neck. "God, thank you for saving those animals. Thank you for equipping Denny and Gail to take them. And . . ."

Jodi stood up and walked to the window. She looked toward the field where Solomon was standing with Lady and Beau. "Father, please give me wisdom to know what to say when Gail calls. Could this have been your plan all along? To add another horse to our herd? Is that even something we could do right now?"

Jodi's prayer trailed off as she thought through the logistics of adding another horse—especially a young horse with a traumatic past. As she walked out the door of the office, several cars were pulling into the parking lot. Her team of volunteers had arrived to help with the afternoon sessions. Jodi had only taken a few steps when her phone rang. Thinking it was Ty, she didn't even look at the number before answering.

"Hi, is this Jodi Stuber?" a woman asked.

Jodi cleared her throat. "It is," she hesitated, wondering how to politely get rid of the telemarketer.

"Jodi, this is Gail Sprague. I hope you don't mind my calling, but Kathy gave me your number."

Jodi hadn't anticipated Gail calling so soon. She had barely had time to give the matter any thought. And yet, she was excited to speak with her.

"Gail, I couldn't believe it when Kathy told me that you and Denny were the ones who have been fostering the rescued horses. Ty and I have been praying for you for months, although I didn't know who we were praying for until about twenty minutes ago. Thank you so much for giving those horses a second chance."

"It has been such a wonderful experience. A hard one for sure, but we're so glad we could help out. Which actually brings me to the reason for my call. I'm sure Kathy told you a little bit about our mare in need of a home?"

"She did, but I'd love to hear more."

Kathy described the dark bay pony they had been calling Sugar. "She was understandably skittish and fearful at first, but she eventually grew more comfortable. A part of me would love to keep her, but since we decided to keep the oldest mare and her foal here for a while longer, we realized that was all we could handle. It will be best to find Sugar a new home."

"Gail, thank you for thinking of us," Jodi said earnestly. "It means so much to know that we have been on your heart. I will never forget your generosity all those years ago and your kindness now in caring for those horses." Jodi sat on a tree stump between her house and HopeWell. "I am going to need to talk to Ty and my HopeWell team to see if we can accommodate Sugar. If it were up to me, HopeWell would be a refuge for all the horses in the world that needed a home, but as we both know, we can't rescue them all." Even as Jodi said the words, she wished she *could* actually save them all. "Can I think and pray about it overnight?"

Gail assured her it would be just fine and reiterated that there was no pressure to say yes—HopeWell had simply been at the top of her list. Jodi thanked her again before saying goodbye. After eating a quick snack and calling Ty to tell him about the pony in need of a home, Jodi joined Linda at the arena for two sessions. The first was with a fourteen-year-old girl named Hannah who was struggling to fit in at school and battling intense loneliness.

As they toured the ranch, the quiet girl kept gravitating toward Chebar, Hopewell's oldest horse. Chebar, and several other mares, had been donated to HopeWell a year after Solomon arrived. Early on, her gentle nature made her well-suited to work with the kids.

"Why is that horse all alone?" Hannah asked.

Jodi explained that the thirty-two-year-old horse needed specialized care. "Chebar has several teeth missing so we have to soak her food in water to make it easier for her to swallow and digest. She also needs extra time to eat . . . without having to worry about other horses chasing her away and stealing her food. So we moved her to her own little field adjoining the larger pasture."

"Can I go in there and say hi to her?" Hannah asked hesitantly.

Jodi opened the gate, and Hannah spent forty-five minutes in the pasture standing with Chebar. Jodi and Linda were nearby but gave the girl space to simply be present with the horse.

When it was time to leave, Hannah asked, "Can I do this again next week?"

Jodi smiled. "Absolutely."

As they walked back to the parking lot, Hannah began to

share a little about the loneliness she had been feeling at school since her best friend had moved away. While Jodi listened, she was grateful that God had worked through Chebar. Many would think an elderly horse didn't have much to offer the world, but Chebar proved them wrong. Her presence and companionship were just what a lonely, wounded soul needed most.

As Jodi waved goodbye to Hannah, she glanced at her watch. She and Linda had fifteen minutes before their next session. They would be working with a ten-year-old boy named Michael whose father had recently returned from his fourth deployment. Michael had been at the ranch once before for an introductory session. The boy had seemed to enjoy meeting the different animals, but he had barely said more than five words the entire visit.

Jodi hoped today's visit would be a positive experience for Michael, but she was struggling to stay focused. Her mind kept wandering back to Sugar. *Could we take on a new horse? How can we say yes? How can we possibly say no?*

"Are you okay?" Linda asked as they walked back into the arena.

Jodi nodded, mentally chiding herself for being so distracted. "Oh, sorry. I'm fine. Just lost in my thoughts," she said, forcing a smile. "So how do you think that session went?"

Linda's prolonged silence forced Jodi to turn around.

"Nice try," Linda said. "I think that session went very well. Hannah made some real progress with Chebar, and I'm hopeful we'll be able to dive deeper at her next visit. However . . . at this moment I am far more concerned about you. You've been distracted all afternoon. Something is weighing on you. Would you like to talk about it?"

Having a trained therapist for a friend and coworker is both great and annoying, Jodi thought.

"Really, I'm fine," Jodi assured her. "Just thinking about a phone call from this morning."

She told Linda about the horse in need of a home, the connection she had to Denny and Gail, and all that Gail had said about the little mare.

"It all sounds good," Jodi concluded, "but would it *be* good for HopeWell? Will Sugar even be trainable given the trauma she's endured?"

Linda, who had been sitting on a picnic table while Jodi recounted the phone call, stood up the moment Jodi was done.

"That is a lot to think about. And I completely understand your hesitancy. It would be a big adjustment for everyone." Linda paused for a moment. "But given the fact that so many of the people we serve come from difficult—even abusive—situations, I bet many people will resonate with Sugar's background . . . maybe even be encouraged by her resilience."

As always, Linda helped Jodi see a situation from a different perspective.

Thirty minutes later, Jodi and Linda stood in the middle of the arena with Michael and Solomon. After being reintroduced to the horses out in the field, Michael had gravitated toward the chestnut gelding who had greeted the boy at the gate when they entered. Michael now stood quietly beside Solomon, running a currycomb along his back.

Michael had watched Jodi carefully as she showed him the proper way to hold the brush. He studied her every movement, even mimicking her motions as she demonstrated how to brush in long strokes along Solomon's back. Michael took the brush from Jodi's hand and stepped silently up to Solomon. With his furrowed brow and the tip of his tongue poking out from between his teeth, Michael was the picture of concentration as he brushed the horse exactly as Jodi had shown him.

"Michael, you're doing a great job on Solomon's coat," Jodi praised after several minutes. Her jubilant voice rang out in the otherwise silent arena. "Just be careful near his back end. He has a sore back there from a horsefly bite that is still healing."

The boy's head jerked up as she spoke. The currycomb fell from his hand, and he backed away from the horse. Jodi was startled by his reaction and so was Solomon, whose ears and head were raised and turned toward the boy with apprehension. Linda saw the moment as the opportunity she had been waiting for.

"Michael, you're safe. It's okay," Linda reassured him. "Did something scare you? Will you tell us what happened?"

Michael's gaze remained fixed on Solomon. The boy appeared to be waiting for something—something that seemed to cause him great anxiety. Finally, he spoke.

"Is he okay?" Michael nodded in Solomon's direction. "Does he want me to go now?"

"Why would Solomon want you to go?" Linda gently inquired.

Michael glanced in Jodi's direction.

"How does Solomon look to you, Michael?" Linda asked.

Michael's attention returned to the horse.

"Okay, I guess?"

"What makes him seem okay?" Linda asked. "What do his

eyes look like? What is he doing with his mouth? What are his ears doing?"

"His eyes are . . . kind of black. And round. His mouth is big, with little whiskers poking out everywhere." Michael stepped closer to Solomon, leaning in for a better look at the horse's mouth. "It kinda looks like he's smiling a little."

Michael's own lips lifted slightly, the closest thing to a smile Jodi had seen on the boy's face. "His ears are standing up like little tents on his head." Michael paused. "Does that mean he's okay? Does he want me to keep brushing him?"

Jodi's heart swelled with affection for the timid—and perceptive—boy. She glanced at Linda, who nodded.

"Michael," Jodi said softly, "you just described a very happy horse. Solomon might have been a little surprised when you jumped back, but he's very happy to be here, and his posture—the way he's standing and how he looks—is telling us that he likes you brushing him."

Michael's lips parted in a genuine smile. "Oh good," he sighed. He picked up the currycomb off the ground and added, "I thought maybe the noise scared him or that I got too close to his sore and that he was going to kick me or something."

"What noise did you think scared him?" Linda probed.

Michael cast a quick look to Jodi but didn't answer.

"Quiet seems to be important to you, Michael. Is that right?"

Michael nodded, his eyes looking far older than his ten years.

"What happens when it's not quiet?"

Jodi was standing in front of Solomon and reached out her hand to stroke his neck.

Michael kept his gaze on his well-worn sneakers. "My dad's head hurts."

"Does your dad's head hurt a lot?" Linda asked, following the boy's lead.

Michael chewed his bottom lip. "Only when I'm loud. Or when there's loud noises outside like fireworks or garbage trucks."

"What happens when your dad's head hurts?" Linda continued.

Michael dug the toe of his shoe into the dirt floor.

"He yells." Michael paused. He shoved his toe deeper into the dirt. "And sometimes he throws things at the wall."

He stared at the sore on Solomon's back. Jodi wanted to say something comforting to the boy, but Linda gave her a subtle wave. Several minutes later, with his gaze still focused on Solomon's sore, Michael whispered, "And sometimes when my dad's head really hurts, his whole body shakes and he lies down on the floor and put his hands over his ears."

Jodi bit the inside of her cheek.

"What does it *feel* like to see your daddy like that?"

"Kinda scary."

"That does sound scary," Linda replied. "Can I tell you something about Solomon?"

Michael nodded, meeting Linda's gaze.

"Ms. Jodi has spent a lot of time training him not to be afraid of loud noises. It's taken a while, but Solomon doesn't mind loud noises anymore. And he really seems to like the noises kids make because those noises mean he gets to play with his friends."

"It's true," Jodi said, picking up on Linda's cue. "Solomon is very used to loud noises. So you can let all of your loud out while you're here. How does that sound?"

A shy smile brightened Michael's face. "Good."

Jodi knew she and Linda would have their work cut out for them as they would walk with Michael through what it meant to live with someone dealing with post-traumatic stress disorder. They would talk about coping strategies, break big concepts like emotional regulation into bite-sized, kid-friendly pieces, and practice living within healthy boundaries. But as she watched Michael begin once again rubbing the brush along Solomon's back, she realized that the most important thing they could offer Michael was a safe place to simply be a kid. Even if just for an hour.

After walking Michael back to his mother, Jodi and Linda made a few notes and plans for his next visit, and then Jodi headed home. She was exhausted, but after dinner she and Ty sat at the kitchen table. She talked about Sugar and the laundry list of reasons she was nervous to say yes to Gail. Ty didn't say anything until Jodi finished and sat back in her chair.

"When do you have to give Gail an answer?"

"I told her I would call her tomorrow."

"It sounds like taking in Sugar could be a good thing, but I know it's a big decision. So let's sleep on it and trust God to show us what to do."

After praying together, Jodi headed upstairs. While she lay in bed, her mind kept drifting to an image of the desperate horses. Did they look up at the starlit sky each night and long for rescue? For mercy? Did they wait in hopeful expectation each morning, wondering if food would come? How long did it take for the first one's spirit to break? Could the damage be repaired?

Jodi fell asleep with those questions on her mind and a

prayer for wisdom in her heart. That night she dreamed of a dark bay mare with a wide white blaze that extended from her forehead to her nostrils. In the dream, Jodi was walking the mare around HopeWell. She woke up smiling and joked to Ty that when you go to bed thinking about horses, apparently you will dream about them too.

15

WITH A FULL DAY of administrative tasks and sessions to prepare for, Jodi went straight to the HopeWell office after feeding the animals. Having prayed most of the morning about whether to add a new horse to the herd, Jodi was starting to feel a peace about saying yes. Yet she still had some doubts.

"Lord, if you want me to say yes, will you confirm that to me in some way today?"

Resolving to leave the matter in God's capable hands, Jodi spent the morning replying to several emails and catching up on paperwork. She had just finished jotting down notes to share with Linda later that day, when her computer dinged with an incoming email from Gail. The subject line read "Our sweet Sugar."

When Jodi clicked on the email, she expected to read more

information about the horse. But what she discovered caused her jaw to drop. Staring back at her from the computer screen was a photo of a dark bay horse with a wide white blaze running from her forehead to her nose. The horse she had dreamed about last night.

"How in the world . . . ," Jodi murmured, struggling to take her eyes off the photo. Gail was apologizing for not sending Jodi a photo of Sugar the day before. She thanked Jodi for the work she was doing at HopeWell and told her to take her time making a decision. Jodi was still staring at the photo when Amanda walked into her office.

"Good morning. You look like you've already been hard at work this morning. Jodi?" she asked, concern evident in her voice. "Is everything all right?"

Her question broke through Jodi's fog.

"I'm sorry. I was just . . . uh . . . I got an email. I think God just sent me an email." Jodi choked out a laugh. "I mean, I know God didn't actually email me. But earlier this morning I asked him for a sign, for confirmation about something. And the email I just received feels like pretty clear confirmation."

Jodi told Amanda about the phone calls, the decision she had to make, and the dream she had last night.

"Whoa," Amanda said, her eyes wide. "I think you're right." Amanda looked over Jodi's shoulder at the screen. "I've always wondered what God's email address is. You should definitely email him back!"

When Amanda left to start her workday, Jodi called Ty to fill him in on the latest developments.

"Well, sounds to me like we're getting another horse."

"I think so too."

Now that she had talked things over with Ty, she quickly dialed Gail's number.

"Jodi, I didn't expect to hear from you so soon."

"To be honest, I didn't think you would either. But you see . . ." She hesitated. *Will Gail think I'm crazy if I tell her about my dream?* It didn't really matter. It had happened, and it was worth sharing. "Gail, you might think this sounds crazy . . . but last night I had a dream about Sugar."

Jodi proceeded to tell Gail about her dream—and about her prayer earlier that morning.

"That is remarkable, Jodi."

"It really is. And I truly believe that it was God making it clear that we should add Sugar to the HopeWell herd."

The rest of the call was spent making plans for Ty and Jodi to meet Sugar two weeks later.

"So let me get this straight," Ty said later that night, his eyes wide with feigned exasperation. "You made plans—on our wedding anniversary—to go meet a horse?"

"Oh no! Did you make reservations for us at that expensive new restaurant?" She fought to keep an expression of hopeful surprise on her face but lost her battle when Ty's face went white. She had wanted to tease her husband, not give him a panic attack! "I'm kidding!" she blurted out. "You know I'd rather meet a horse and have a peanut butter sandwich with you than eat a fancy dinner in a stuffy restaurant." The look of relief on Ty's face made her laugh out loud.

∪

"Why are they cleaning that field?" Shawn asked Jodi several days later as they walked to the pasture to get Solomon.

Jodi still couldn't get over the changes in Shawn. In the eight months since his last session, the now sixteen-year-old had grown at least three inches, and his voice had dropped an entire octave. He had come so far since his first visit to HopeWell more than four years ago. Shawn's mother credited a great deal of her son's progress to the bond he had formed with Solomon—and to the acceptance and opportunities he had received at HopeWell. Jodi looked toward the small field where several volunteers were shoveling, raking, and cleaning the water trough.

"They are getting the field ready for a new horse who might be coming to live at HopeWell next week."

Shawn suddenly stopped.

"Solomon lives here!"

"Solomon will stay here. This is Solomon's home, and we love him very much," Jodi reassured him.

"I love him," Shawn declared.

"Yes, you do. You are a good friend to Solomon."

"I am Solomon's friend," Shawn repeated. "Solomon is my horse brother."

Jodi's heart swelled. "Come on. Let's go get him."

As Jodi watched the teenager lead Solomon from the field to the hitching post and begin grooming him, an idea began to form. *We should invite Shawn to become an equine care volunteer.* It had become clear to her, toward the end of last year's season, that Shawn's sessions had become less about his personal growth and more about him simply enjoying being around Solomon. Perhaps it was time to graduate Shawn to a different role and purpose at the ranch.

Jodi shared the idea with Shawn's mother, Carol, who

beamed at the thought of her son "graduating" from sessions to a role that would give him some responsibility. "Anything that will keep him part of the HopeWell community sounds good to me." At first, Shawn didn't seem to understand the difference between sessions and becoming a volunteer.

"You will still visit with Solomon, but now you will help us take care of him—and some of the other horses too. How does that sound?"

"Good!" Shawn exclaimed, pumping his fist in the air.

Jodi knew it would take a while—and a lot of patience—to help Shawn transition from sessions to a volunteer role, but she had no doubt he could do it. And she suspected he would do it with a level of excellence and devotion that would inspire everyone at HopeWell.

U

"So . . . what do you think?" Ty asked Jodi. It was the morning of their anniversary, and they stood near the eastern edge of the HopeWell property.

"What do I think of what exactly?" Ty had all but dragged her from the house, saying he had an anniversary present for her.

"That!" Ty said, pointing triumphantly to a rectangular section of ground, marked off by white spray paint.

"Um . . . it's nice ground?"

"Oh, you of little vision," Ty chided. "That *ground*, as you so unimaginatively called it, is the beginning of a garden. But not just *any* garden," Ty added, taking Jodi's hand. "It is going to be a memorial garden—a living memorial to Hope."

Jodi's eyes widened, and she allowed her tears to speak the words she could not get out. A year after Hope's death, they had talked about the idea of some kind of memorial or tribute. But then things had started taking off at HopeWell, life picked up speed, and the idea had been all but forgotten. Until now.

Jodi stepped into Ty's embrace. "It's absolutely perfect. Thank you."

Jodi walked the perimeter of the twelve-by-twelve garden. As she did, she envisioned flowers, shrubs, benches, a birdbath, and a whimsical statue or two. Jodi's eyes sparkled with the possibilities. "Can we start on it now?"

Ty put his hands on her shoulders. "Easy there. In case you've forgotten, we have a filly to pick up today."

"Oh my goodness! I forgot! What time is it? We've got to get ready."

Jodi turned and started toward the house. She stopped after three steps, ran back to Ty, and threw her arms around him.

"Thank you for the best anniversary gift ever! Our *Hope Garden.*"

"Gail, she is beautiful," Jodi whispered, several hours later.

The young mare eyed them cautiously. Jodi knew that only time and consistent care would earn Sugar's trust.

"You're okay, Sugar," Denny said quietly. "Jodi and Ty are good people. And they are going to take excellent care of you."

The affection the man had for the pony was evident on his face. But he and Gail had been adamant that they wanted their Sugar to have the opportunity to make a difference in the world at HopeWell.

Denny walked Sugar to the trailer. Sugar put on the brakes when they got within six feet. Ty had opened the back door to reveal a feed bucket with grain and oats hanging on one side and a full bag of hay on the other. As Denny gently and slowly guided Sugar up the ramp and clipped the trailer tie on her halter, a memory of loading Solomon all those years ago flitted through Jodi's mind. She hoped the two of them would get along.

Everyone breathed a collective sigh of relief when Sugar went right for the grain. Ty closed and secured the door. Minutes later, they were making their way down the Spragues' winding driveway. Ty looked at Jodi and winked.

"So apparently the traditional gift for a twenty-fourth wedding anniversary is a horse?" he teased.

"And a garden," she added.

"I feel so sorry for all those poor wives who are forced to endure roses and fancy dinners on their anniversary when they could have dirt and livestock instead."

Jodi couldn't have agreed more.

16

Aside from a chorus of curious and excited whinnies when they arrived, it was a quiet homecoming for the newest member of the HopeWell herd. Given the mare's history, and her limited experience with humans, Jodi had decided to ask only Amanda and Tania to be the welcoming committee.

As Ty opened the trailer, Jodi prayed Sugar would unload easily but prepared herself for the likely possibility that she would not. The moment the door opened, the horse whinnied. The sound sent the nearby herd into a frenzy. Whinnies were thrown back and forth, in what sounded to Jodi like the horse version of a Marco Polo game. Jodi was preparing to back the mare out of the trailer using her halter and lead rope, but to her surprise, Sugar spun in a half-circle, turned, and walked right down the ramp.

At the foot of the ramp, Sugar stopped, facing the large pasture where the herd was looking at her. Someone gave a loud whiny—Jodi suspected it was Solomon. The mare whinnied back, and the game of Marco Polo was back on. The whinnies quieted as Jodi led Sugar to her temporary home in the small adjoining field.

The walk went smoothly—until the gate got away from Tania and slammed against the lock. The mare's front legs came off the ground, and her eyes widened with fear.

"Shhh . . . you're okay," Jodi soothed, working to keep the pony under control. "You're okay, you're okay."

Sugar's panic rippled through the herd. Bubba Jack and Beau started running, while Destiny and Samson whinnied their concern. Solomon, however, stood still, his head high and his ears pointed in the mare's direction. Jodi watched him for a moment, concerned that maybe he wasn't feeling well. She had heard him coughing earlier that morning, but thankfully he seemed to be just fine now. Jodi hated that his asthma had been so bad this year. Doctor Brenda had been out two weeks ago and adjusted one of his medications. She had also advised against strenuous exercise for the horse, saying that galloping or heavy exercise could put excess pressure on his lungs. Thankfully, Solomon didn't seem to mind his slower-paced sessions, and Jodi was hopeful the new regimen would keep his symptoms at bay.

While Jodi had been studying Solomon, their new mare had calmed down enough to be led around the perimeter of the field. Jodi spoke softly to her as they walked. She told her about her equine neighbors and about some of the humans she would meet at the ranch. She stopped at the water trough and hay bag to give the pony time to get familiar with their location. When their tour was complete, Jodi removed the halter, gave the mare a gentle pat, and let her go.

"Anything you want us to do?" Amanda asked, as Jodi gently closed the gate.

"Pray that she settles in quickly; that the herd will accept her; and that we will be able to show her a kinder side of humanity. And let's ask God to heal that precious girl's wounded spirit—and to pour out his favor and mercy."

Mercy.

Jodi turned to Ty, Amanda, and Tania.

"What if we call her Mercy?"

Everyone agreed that it was the perfect name for a horse who had faced the worst life had to offer—and was still standing. Mercy was a survivor. And in many ways her new name felt like a promise Jodi was making to her. A promise she vowed to keep.

After Amanda and Tania left for the day, and Ty went to take measurements for the Hope Garden, Jodi approached Mercy by herself. "What do you think of your new home, Mercy?"

Mercy flicked an ear in Jodi's direction but kept her focus on the neighboring herd. Jodi knew what the pony needed most was time to just be. And so with a whispered prayer of protection for Mercy and the herd, Jodi walked to the large pasture to check the water levels. Solomon made his way over to greet her.

"Hi, Solly. You seem to be feeling better. What do you think of our new girl?"

Solomon exhaled loudly.

"Do me a favor and look out for her. Mercy's been through a lot and could really use a protector and friend out here."

After quietly closing the pasture gate, Jodi turned back for one last peek at Mercy. The dark-coated mare was standing in the middle of her field. And standing across from her, on the other side of the fence, was Solomon.

"Good boy, Solly."

17

"PUT YOUR SHOULDERS BACK a little, Michael," Jodi said in their session with Solomon, two days after bringing Mercy home. "That's good. When riding, you want to make sure you're sitting up as straight as you can. How's that feel?"

"Really good."

"He's a natural," Linda observed.

Michael had been hesitant to ride, but when Jodi made it clear that the choice was his—he decided to give it a try. After a wobbly start trying to get his leg over the saddle, he had settled in and seemed to be thoroughly enjoying himself on Solomon. Jodi talked to him about proper form, how to hold the reins, and how to use rein and leg pressure to ask the horse to turn. Michael absorbed her instructions like a thirsty sponge.

"You did a fantastic job, Michael," Jodi praised as she helped the boy climb off Solomon's back.

"That was fun! Can I do it again next time?"

"Of course you can," Jodi and Linda answered together.

"Woo-hoo!" Michael shouted, taking a giant leap off the top of the mounting block and sticking the landing on the sandy ground.

As quickly as his jubilant outburst had come, it vanished. Jodi watched as regret and fear shadowed Michael's young face. His hazel eyes flew to the horse.

"Look at Solomon, Michael," Jodi said. "What is his body saying to you?"

Michael chewed his bottom lip while he studied the horse. "His eyes are saying 'I see you.'"

Michael looked at Jodi for approval. She smiled and nodded.

"What else is Solomon saying to you?" Linda encouraged.

"His lips are moving a lot . . . so I think he's saying, 'I'm hungry.' Oh wait! Ms. Jodi said that when horses do that it means they're thinking, right? So maybe Solomon is thinking? Probably about food!"

"Anything else?"

Michael took a tentative step toward Solomon who turned his head.

"His ears are standing up tall. They look . . . sort of happy. Maybe he's saying, 'I'm happy you're here.'"

"Solomon does look like a very happy horse," Jodi confirmed.

"What do you think Solomon thinks about you being loud?" Linda asked gently.

Michael paused. "I think . . . he likes it."

"I think he does too. Solomon doesn't seem to mind loud

noises at all. But we just got a new horse—her name is Mercy—and she seems to be very scared of loud noises. Especially the noise the gate makes when it slams closed. I think it's going to take a long time for us to help her learn not to be afraid of our gates and other loud sounds."

"Can I meet Mercy?"

Jodi looked at Linda, who nodded. They agreed it was a wonderful idea.

"After Mercy settles in a little more, I think she would like that very much," Jodi replied.

After putting Solomon back in the field, Jodi and Linda walked Michael toward the pavilion where Jodi assumed his mother would be waiting. However, Michael went past the pavilion and headed toward the parking lot.

"My dad's picking me up. He told me to meet him at the car." Michael hesitated. "He . . . um . . . doesn't really like horses too much. There he is," he said, pointing to a white sedan.

A man with short brown hair rolled down the passenger window and waved. "Hi, I'm Chad. Thanks for having Mikey out today. He really likes it here."

"Nice to meet you, Chad. We absolutely love having Michael here." Jodi paused then added, "And we'd love to show you around—maybe give you the grand tour—next time you come."

"Yeah, sure. Maybe next time."

Michael waved as the car pulled out of the parking lot. Moments later the two were gone.

"Think Michael's dad will take me up on that offer?" Jodi asked Linda.

"I don't know. I kind of doubt it. But I think the best thing we can do right now is give that little boy a safe place to be carefree. Besides, I'm not sure we would even be equipped to serve veterans. Remember last year when that administrator from the VA hospital came out to volunteer with his daughter's class? We talked to him about a possible partnership and thought it could be great to offer services to our country's heroes. But remember how he shot down the idea?"

Jodi certainly remembered. She and Linda had attended an equine guided therapy conference where they heard heartbreaking statistics about mental health problems and suicide in the veteran population. As Jodi had listened to the promising stories of veterans finding help through equine programs, she had started to dream about HopeWell offering a similar program. The two of them returned to HopeWell eager to start making plans. But after the man from the VA had said how difficult it would be to gain the veterans' trust, since no one at HopeWell had served in the military, Jodi had let go of the idea. Who was she to take on something so big? Who was she to think she could offer anything to men and women who were willing to die to protect her freedom?

But now, as she pictured Chad and Michael, a real father and son who needed help, she found herself wishing she hadn't given up on the idea so quickly.

After seeing Linda off, Jodi decided to check on Mercy one last time. She was at her feed bag, pulling clumps of hay through the net. She watched Jodi approach but turned her backside toward the gate when Jodi put her hand on the latch.

"You don't want anything to do with me, do you?" Jodi asked softly. "I don't blame you. You take your time."

Remembering how Mercy had reacted to the gate slamming

shut that first day, Jodi took great care to close it quietly as she entered. Mercy's ears were pinned back—the tips of them pointing toward Jodi. While Mercy's posture would communicate anger and possibly even an eminent attack in most horses, Jodi had studied the little mare enough over the past forty-eight hours to recognize her stance as one of fear.

Mercy stood frozen in place. Jodi longed to walk to her. To stroke her neck and show her every kindness. Yet she knew that her attempts would not be well received. Jodi resolved to become a student of Mercy, to learn how to best show her the love and compassion she deserved.

"I won't push. I'll just stay close while you heal."

Jodi stood near the gate for several minutes—not talking, not staring, just being present. Minutes later, she gingerly lifted the latch and softly closed the gate behind her. Mercy's ears rose, then she lowered her head. In that moment, Jodi realized that sometimes the kindest thing you can do for someone is keep your word.

18

JODI POUNDED A METAL TRELLIS STAKE into the soft earth. She adjusted the mallet in her hand, retrieved another stake, and repeated the process. Satisfied that the trellis was secure, she inhaled deeply. A light breeze heralded the promise of summer. Jodi could almost smell the flowers that would soon fill Hope Garden. With thirty minutes to spare before Jessica and Richard arrived for a Friday family dinner, she figured she had just enough time to place the three trellises she had bought the previous weekend. Jodi loved flowering vines and wanted to incorporate some into the garden. She had just finished securing the final stake when she heard Jessica. "Hey, Mom? Are you out here?"

"Over here, sweetheart."

Jessica stopped and surveyed the garden. "You sure have gotten a lot done in a week. It looks great!"

Jodi turned around to see the garden's progress from her daughter's eyes. Jodi had been so focused on how much they still had left to do that she hadn't stopped to enjoy everything that they had accomplished. She gave Jessica a brief tour, highlighting the different areas and sections and what they had planned for each.

"I love this so much, Mom," Jessica said. "I'd like to plant something for my little sister too."

Four years ago, Jodi couldn't have imagined having a moment like this with Jessica. Remembering the countless prayers she had spoken, many of which had been prayed near this very spot, Jodi offered a silent *thank you* to the One who seemed to delight in the impossible.

"I think that would be absolutely wonderful, Jess," Jodi replied, giving her daughter a hug.

"Also . . ." Jessica hesitated, looking a little unsure. "The reason I'm a little early is because I wanted to invite you to something as kind of a late anniversary present."

Jodi enthusiastically nodded.

"Mom, you haven't even heard what it is yet," Jessica said, laughing.

"It doesn't matter," Jodi replied. "As long as it's with you, I'm in!"

Jessica's face lit up.

"Well, the Curtis family is opening up their farm next Saturday to anyone who wants to learn about organic farming practices. And since you're getting more into all of that, I thought you might like to go."

Can a human heart burst from happiness? Jodi wondered.

"Oh, Jess, that sounds like a perfect way to spend a day.

Thank you for thinking of that. It will be a wonderful way to kick off Memorial Day weekend."

The two agreed Jessica would pick Jodi up at the ranch at 9:00 a.m., which would give Jodi plenty of time to feed the animals and get herself ready. As they walked to the house together, they chatted about Jessica's job, the nice young man named James she had started dating, and Mercy, who had just been moved into the large pasture.

"So Solomon looks out for her, huh? That's really cool."

"He does, and it is," Jodi replied. "I've even seen him put himself between her and the herd twice now—once when she was in the small field, and then again the first day she was in the large pasture with the others."

Jodi began to describe the scene as it replayed in her mind. "After a few hours of engaging in their typical hierarchy shenanigans, Mercy had grown tired. I was so nervous about the whole thing that I was ready to go in and put her back in the small field. But before I could do anything, Solomon positioned himself between the herd and Mercy and planted his feet. Within minutes, the rest of the herd stopped moving. And Mercy was able to rest."

"And that was it? They all just stopped chasing her?"

"Well, that was it for a while," Jodi said with a wink. "There were still some shenanigans over the next twenty-four hours, but Solomon seemed to keep things from going too far."

"That's incredible, Mom."

"It really is," Jodi agreed. "It makes me wonder if he remembers how the herd treated him when he first arrived, and he decided he's not going to tolerate such things for Mercy."

"Could that actually happen?" Jessica sounded both intrigued and skeptical. "Can horses really do things like that?"

"Truthfully? I don't know . . . probably not," she confessed. "But that's how I like to think about it. And besides, Solomon is so different from any horse I've ever known that I honestly wouldn't put it past him."

"Hey!" Ty's voice bellowed from the house. "Are you two gonna stay out there gabbing all night? You have two hungry men in here!"

"Some things never change." Jodi laughed, following Jessica into the house.

19

SATURDAY DAWNED BRIGHT AND CLEAR. *Thank you for such a beautiful day, Lord.*

Jodi had gotten up just before sunrise, and after a quick breakfast, she walked over to the ranch to begin the morning routine. She prayed as she went about her tasks, pausing from time to time to inhale the warm spring air—air that felt saturated with the promise of new beginnings.

"Who's hungry?" she called out as she entered the pasture.

A chorus of nickers and snorts replied. Jodi smiled every time she saw the horses line themselves up at mealtimes. It was the same at the water trough. Years ago, when Ty had first noticed the formation, he said they looked like elementary school students in the cafeteria line.

Jodi fed Solomon first. He preferred to eat closest to the water trough, which Jodi assumed was equivalent to sitting at the head of a large banquet table. After delivering all the meals, Jodi began to top off their water. As the water line inched its way higher up the rubber trough, the peace of the moment warmed her heart. The only sounds she heard were those of the horses eating and bees buzzing in search of pollen. Only a few times in her life had she ever remembered feeling such a strong sense of contentment. *Thank you, Father.*

The moment seemed to envelop her soul like a heavenly embrace. Not wanting to leave that embrace—but also not wanting to miss her day with Jessica—she knew it was time to go. She started for the gate but stopped and walked back to Solomon. She wanted to check his breathing before she left.

"I forgot to check that nose of yours."

She stroked his muzzle, focusing on his breathing as she did. His nostrils looked fairly normal. Only a little drainage. She couldn't detect any signs of labored breathing. And she hadn't heard him cough this morning.

"Hi, buddy. You sound much better." She leaned her forehead against his for a moment, and then gave him a kiss on the nose. "I'm going to be out for a bit with Jessica. So keep an eye on things for me." Solomon seemed to nod his head in agreement and turned his attention back to his hay.

Jodi hurried home to change. While she was getting dressed, Tania called to ask if she could bring her daughter and her daughter's friend by the ranch.

"The girls had a sleepover, and they can't wait to see the horses," Tania explained. "We won't stay long, but I wanted to check with you first."

Jodi told Tania that she was spending the day with Jessica, but that Tania and the girls were welcome anytime. She turned up the volume on the radio station playing one of her favorite worship songs as she finished dressing, and after a quick swipe of lip balm, she headed downstairs and out the door just as Jessica pulled up.

"Hey, Mom."

"Good morning, sweetheart. Thank you again for arranging this. I am so excited!"

Jessica smiled. "Me too."

Jodi studied her daughter's profile as Jessica started down the driveway. *When did my little girl become such a strong and beautiful woman?*

"I guess Solomon must have had a really big breakfast, huh?" Jessica said with a laugh as they drove parallel to the large field.

"Hmm?" Jodi replied, digging through her purse. "I could have sworn I put my phone in here. . . . Oh, there it is." Jodi pulled her phone from the inner pocket of her purse and dropped it in Jessica's cup holder. "Sorry, honey. What did you say?"

"Oh nothing. Solomon is just lying down in the middle of the field—at least I think it was Solomon. I can't really tell them all apart. Anyway, I just said he must have had a big breakfast. You know, like dad on pancake Saturdays."

Jodi smiled at the image of Ty sound asleep with a belly full of pancakes. "Well, I guess a post-breakfast nap is one of the many perks of being the herd leader."

The two women fell into easy conversation as they made their way to the farm. Jodi loved hearing Jessica talk about her dreams and goals. And the more she listened to her talk about James, the more Jodi suspected he might play a significant role in Jessica's future dreams.

Fifteen minutes into the drive, Jodi's phone rang. Tania's name flashed on the screen. Jodi looked at Jessica as she answered. This was supposed to be their mother-daughter day. Jodi couldn't imagine why Tania was calling, but she would find out quickly.

"Jodi, something's wrong with the fence. It's broken near the water trough, and several posts are crooked and bent. I'm afraid the horses might get out."

"What?" Jodi was dumbfounded. *I was in the field less than an hour ago. What in the world could have happened?*

"Okay . . . ," Jodi stammered, trying to think quickly. "Turn off the electricity to the fence and do your best to jerry-rig the post so the horses can't get out. I won't be gone long." The moment the last words flew out of her mouth, Jodi looked at Jessica.

"Actually, Tania, Ty will be home soon. I'll ask him to fix it as soon as he gets there."

"Okay, I'll see what I can do."

Jodi ended the call and dropped her phone back in the cup holder.

"Sorry about that," she said. "I have no idea what could have happened to the fence, but Tania's on it."

"I know it takes a lot to keep HopeWell running, and you need to know when there's a problem." Jessica started up the driveway to the Curtis farm. "I'm just glad we were able to do this together."

"Me too."

The women had just stepped out of the car when Jodi's phone rang again. *Tania.* She was tempted to let it go to voice-mail, but if Tania needed help dealing with the fence, she had to contact some other volunteers. Jodi gave Jessica an apologetic look and answered.

"Jodi . . ." Tania's voice sounded odd. "Solomon is dead!"

Wait . . . what? WHAT! Jodi didn't know if she had spoken the words aloud or screamed them in her head.

"I just found him lying in the field. I thought he was sleeping, but oh, Jodi . . ." Tania's voice broke.

"I'm on my way." Jodi turned to Jessica. "Something happened to Solomon. He's . . ."

Jodi couldn't say the words. Couldn't believe the words. No, she refused to believe them.

"I'll get you home as fast as I can, Mom."

Nothing made sense to Jodi. Nothing felt real. She had just been standing with Solomon in the field, feeling wrapped in a blanket of peace. She would have known if something was wrong. Her body began to shake. Silent tears streamed down her face. Jessica reached over and took hold of her hand. "We'll be home soon."

Jodi saw a resolve on her daughter's face that she had never seen before. It was a resolve that brought Jodi a hint of comfort that allowed her to close her eyes. She tried to pray. But every attempt to ask for strength and help turned into a desperate cry of *Why?* And a protest of *No!*

As they passed the large pasture, Jodi forced herself to look out the window. Her beautiful chestnut gelding was lying there.

"Oh God . . . help," she prayed aloud, feeling pain building in her chest.

Tania's car was in the driveway. *Tania. The girls!* Jodi had forgotten that Tania had young children with her.

"I have to be strong for Tania and the girls," Jodi commanded herself aloud.

"Mom! Look at me. You do *not* have to be strong for anyone. You get to be who you are, okay? I'll be right here with you."

Jodi clutched Jessica's hand.

"We're going to get through this."

Jodi didn't know if the words had come from her lips or Jessica's. But she clung to them. She took a steadying breath and opened her door.

"Oh, Jodi, I am so sorry," Tania cried, running to embrace her.

Jodi hugged her tight and thanked her for being there. The young girl tugged on Jodi's shirt.

"Do you want us to go in there with you?" she asked, pointing to the pasture.

Jodi forced a slight smile. "Thank you, honey, but I'll be okay."

Jodi turned to Jessica. "I need to go see him."

Jessica and Tania nodded, each taking a step back, and gently moving the girls with them. Jodi took a shaky breath and began walking toward the field. Except for the mangled section of fence, nothing seemed out of the ordinary. The herd was scattered about the field grazing or resting. The sky was still a brilliant blue. And the air was still quiet enough to hear bees buzzing. Jodi could almost convince herself that Solomon was just sleeping.

Except he wasn't.

The moment Jodi approached him, his eery stillness caused

her knees to drop. There was no denying that he was gone. Her beloved companion. The horse of her heart. *Oh God, no!*

She buried her face in her hands and sobbed.

"What happened?" she whimpered.

There were no visible marks on him. He didn't look sick. In fact, he looked peaceful. *The injury must be on his other side. When Ty comes home, we will turn him over. Perhaps then we'll have a better idea of what happened.* She replayed the last moments she had shared with Solomon. He had been eating. He had looked healthy. Now she stroked Solomon's neck one last time, then walked back to Jessica and Tania.

"Mom, I am so sorry," Jessica said, burying her head in Jodi's shoulder.

"Me too, baby."

She wiped her eyes on her shirt.

"I need to make some calls. I need to call animal control—or should I call the department of natural resources? I'm not sure. I need to call Dr. Pol or Dr. Brenda. Should I call the marshal? Or the sheriff? We need to find out what happened . . ." Jodi paused for a moment. "I've got to call Ty!"

"Jodi, let me make some phone calls while you wait for Ty. Please. I need to do something," Tania said.

"Mom, I already called Dad. He's on his way. And he asked me to take you home to wait for him."

Jodi nodded. The three women and two girls walked toward the house. Tania hugged Jodi at the door and made her promise to call if she needed her.

"For any reason at all," Tania clarified.

Jodi numbly walked inside and sat on the sofa. Her mind

was racing, yet she was unable to form a coherent thought. Jessica put a glass of water in her hand.

"Take a sip," Jessica ordered. "Why don't you go lie down for a few minutes? I'll wait here for Dad."

Jodi started to protest, but she suddenly felt tired—so very tired.

"I imagine it's going to be a long day," Jessica spoke softly. "You should get some rest while you can."

Jodi nodded, resigned that for the moment there was nothing she could do. After all, he was gone.

Gone.

The word ricocheted through her mind as she made her way upstairs to the bedroom. Barely pausing to kick off her shoes, Jodi fell onto the bed. As numbness gave way to grief, she buried her head in the pillow and screamed.

"Not again!" she wailed into her pillow. "I can't do this again, God! Why? Why would you make me do this again?"

Panic shot through Jodi's heart as she remembered the darkness she had faced in this room seven years ago. She had felt certain that God had sent Solomon to help her find her way out of that darkness. But now he was gone. *How much do I have to lose?* Fear gripped her heart as she awaited the inevitable darkness.

Jodi wept until exhaustion ushered her into a fitful sleep.

"I just don't understand," Jodi said a few hours later as she and Ty stood over Solomon's body. "There's no way that small gash on his leg killed him. What happened?" She swallowed, forcing down the hysteria rising in her throat. "I *need* to know what happened."

Ty had arrived home just as Jodi was stirring from her brief nap. After recapping what she knew, they had walked back to the field. Ty had already moved Solomon's body from the field and turned him over. Jodi had been grateful that she hadn't seen her beautiful chestnut gelding in the loader's bucket.

Now, as Ty and Jodi stood outside the field looking at the small wound on Solomon's leg, Jodi was even more confused. As was the rest of the herd. While the other horses had seemed perfectly content when Jodi had gone running into the field after Tania's call, now they were acting as agitated as she felt. Jodi knew that between the noise of the heavy machinery and the fact that their herd leader had been taken from their field, it would take them quite a while to settle down. Ty studied the ground where the fence was broken.

"See anything?"

"Something . . . ," Ty answered.

As Jodi stood to join him, she heard a car door slam shut, followed by another. The animal control officer and Dr. Brenda were in the parking lot. *How did they know to come?* But then she remembered Tania saying something about making some calls. But it was a holiday weekend. Jodi hadn't expected anyone to come out until Tuesday.

"It's a holiday weekend!" Jodi blurted out.

Dr. Brenda smiled sadly. "But you and I both know death and tragedy have no respect for holidays."

Brenda's presence suddenly felt like a lifeline.

"Jodi, I am so sorry," she said, her eyes filled with compassion.

Jodi offered a simple "thank you" before greeting the animal control officer. She led both Dr. Brenda and the officer to where they had placed Solomon's body.

An hour later, after walking through the field, studying the breaks in the fence, following hoof marks outside the fence, and examining the cuts on Solomon's legs—as well as his recent medical history—Dr. Brenda and the animal control officer were able to offer a possible explanation to what might have happened.

"My best guess is that an animal—likely a wild dog because of the time of day—made its way through the fence and either surprised or tried to attack Solomon," the officer said. "The horse would have reacted, likely rearing up and whinnying the alarm. Based on all the hoof marks in the field, the herd must have gone into panic mode, and in the chaos Solomon bolted through the fence."

Jodi cringed thinking about the fear and pain Solomon must had have felt in that moment.

Brenda picked up on the rest of their theory. "Given the tracks we found running up and down the north side of the pasture and how torn up the grass is, it seems pretty clear that he was galloping at full speed. I suspect that as his adrenaline started to wane, he got tired and turned around to return to his herd."

Jodi found herself both curious and grateful as to why he returned. She knew that as a herd animal, he would have craved the safety of the herd. But the opening he had created when he broke through the fence was fairly small. It would have required him to find the exact location—and walk through an area that had previously shocked him. Jodi tucked the thought away as Dr. Brenda went on.

"I think the stress from the attack—the flood of stress hormones, along with the effects on his heart and lungs from his frantic run—was simply too much for his body. We've known his lungs were compromised from the asthma, and I suspect now that his heart had been as well."

Jodi tried to absorb the information, but all she could think about was how and why Solomon had gone back into the field. She tried to listen to what the animal control officer was telling Ty about recent reports of wild dogs in the area. But her mind refused to cooperate. She kept picturing Solomon lying in the middle of the field with the rest of the herd grazing peacefully around him. *If only the field was closer to the house, I might have heard something. Been there to help,* she lamented silently. As Ty led the animal control officer toward the woods that adjoin their property, Brenda put her hand on Jodi's shoulder.

"You doing okay?" Her eyes were full of kindness as she spoke.

Jodi tried to focus on Brenda's face. "I think so. I just can't stop wondering how or why Solomon went back in the field. None of this makes any sense."

"Come here a minute," Brenda gently ordered, leading Jodi back to the field. Once they arrived, Brenda motioned to the herd. "What do you see?"

"A herd without its leader," Jodi answered bitterly.

"That's right," Brenda said, surprising Jodi. "Now think about how those horses must have been reacting to the attack on their leader."

Jodi shuddered at the image that flew through her mind—Solomon whining in pain and surprise, rearing up in panic, then fleeing for his life. His frantic reaction causing the beast of a dog to run. The rest of the herd would have panicked, and there would have been utter chaos.

"They must have been terrified," Jodi muttered.

"I think so too," Brenda said. "And if there was ever a time they needed their leader, it would have been then, right?"

Jodi's eyes grew rounder. She looked toward where she had found Solomon.

"Jodi," Brenda said, turning to face her, "you've told me several times that no horse has ever loved his herd as much as Solomon loved his." Jodi nodded. "I think there is a very strong possibility that he returned to his herd to calm them down. To ensure they were safe. And possibly to position himself between them and another potential attack."

Brenda paused, waiting for Jodi to look at her. "Jodi, I think Solomon came back to the field to lay down his life for his herd."

Jodi gasped.

What?

She thought about how calm the herd had seemed when she arrived. They had been spread out and grazing around Solomon. She had assumed they had been guarding him. But what if . . . what if they had been drawing comfort and peace *from* him? What if his presence had comforted and relaxed them? A darker thought then entered Jodi's mind. One that made her think of Solomon's return in a different and even more distressing way. *Had the wild dog returned, it surely would have gone for the easy target on the ground—leaving the rest of the herd alone.* Jodi trembled at the thought. She shook her head, trying to dislodge the image from her brain.

"Brenda, do you really think that's possible?" she asked in a whisper.

Even as Jodi asked the question, she felt the answer in her soul. How many times had she witnessed Solomon somehow knowing what another horse or human needed? Whether it was a child in a session, or a horse in need of protection, Solomon had an innate understanding of what was needed from him. *Hadn't he known exactly what I needed, even before I did?*

Of course he would sacrifice himself for the good of the herd.

"I really do," Brenda answered.

"Me too," Jodi replied, pride and sorrow weaving through her heart.

After walking Brenda to her car and thanking her for coming so quickly, Jodi turned to Ty. But before she could say anything, he held his hand up.

"I'm going to move him to the back field. I've already called Bob. He'll come by later this evening." Ty paused. "Do you want to be there?"

Jodi's eyes slid shut. Her chin quivered. Their friend Bob graciously donated his time and his backhoe when they needed to bury a horse. Ty would use the skid steer to carry the horse to the back of their property, which served as an animal cemetery, and Bob would come by in the late afternoon to bury Solomon. Jodi couldn't stand the idea of watching her beloved horse being lowered into the ground. She shook her head.

"No, I can't . . ."

Ty wrapped his arms around her.

"Why don't you go home and let Jessica know what Dr. Brenda said?"

Jodi gratefully took the suggestion he offered.

"Yes," she said, turning toward their house.

"Hey, Jodi," Ty called after she had walked a few steps.

She stopped and turned to face him. "Hmm?"

"I'm really going to miss your handsome stud."

A faint smile crossed Jodi's lips. "He's a . . ." She inhaled a shaky breath, then nodded. "Me too."

20

THE NEXT MORNING Jodi tried to force herself from bed, but an unrelenting heaviness pressed against her like a weighted blanket. A blanket she didn't have the strength or desire to push off. Ty kissed her forehead.

"I'll feed the crew today," he said.

Jodi half-smiled her thanks, turned over, and went back to sleep. She spent most of the day in bed—yearning for the blissful oblivion of sleep, only to be jolted awake by images of wild dogs and stampeding horses. Her phone dinged often with concerned friends and family wanting to check on her. Jodi appreciated their concern, as well as their prayers, but eventually she turned off her phone.

Later that evening Jessica and Richard stopped by for their

annual Memorial Day weekend barbecue—which they had planned weeks ago. Ty had offered to call the kids and cancel, but Jodi refused. She craved a moment of normalcy—even as she resented it. She hosted the patriotic-themed dinner as if on autopilot. Smiling at all the right places and answering every question directed at her.

Yes, she was doing okay.

Yes, Ty was going to fix the fence.

No, they had never seen wild dogs in the area before.

Yes, she was concerned about another attack, but since animal control believed it was an isolated incident, and since the wild dog would have been scared off, they weren't too worried about it happening again.

Jodi was exhausted by early evening. Once the sky grew dark, she pleaded a headache and trudged her way to bed.

"She'll be okay," Jodi heard Ty say as she approached their bedroom. "She's just going to need some time."

A cynical laugh escaped Jodi's lips. Ha! As if time could help. As if time could ever bring someone back! It certainly hadn't brought back Hope.

Fight.

The word—whispered somewhere between her heart and mind—came so suddenly that Jodi froze. The word felt like a command . . . and a promise. But as quickly as it entered her consciousness, it vanished. *Fight? Fight what?* she contemplated while pulling the covers back. *Fight how?* she wondered as she crawled into bed. *Fight who?* she pondered as she laid her head against the pillow. *It's hard enough just to get out of bed, let alone fight anything.* She tried to pray, but her mind kept wandering back to another Memorial Day weekend many years ago when she pounded a bunch of fence posts into the ground. Grief squeezed her heart. Those first fence posts had been planted in pain, and they'd only brought more pain. More loss. More death. Maybe it was time to stop pretending that HopeWell was anything other than a tribute to loss. Too weary to think anymore, Jodi surrendered to sleep.

When she awakened the next morning, Ty was standing over her with a worried expression on his face.

"Good morning. You're up early," she said, forcing a weak smile.

"Jodi, please don't. Don't hide. Don't try to put the mask back on." He lifted her chin to meet his eyes. "Let me help."

"You are." She sat up and rubbed the sleep from her eyes. "I didn't know how I was going to face the herd without Solomon yesterday, but you fed them. Just like I'm guessing you did this morning too. Thank you."

Jodi knew she would have to face Solomon's absence eventually, but she was grateful for the brief reprieve. In her mind, Solomon was still out there—protecting his herd, waiting for her to come visit. Yet, even as she allowed the comforting thought, she knew it was a false reality that would do nothing but delay the inevitable pain she must walk through.

Ty's voice interrupted her thoughts. "I need to head to the hardware store. I was able to temporarily fix the fence the other day, but I need some supplies before I can really fix it. I also noticed a few other weak spots, so if you don't mind, I'm going to work on that today."

"Thanks," she replied, unaware of the monotone sound to her voice.

A thought flashed in her mind.

Mercy.

"Ty? Will you move Mercy to the round pen while you're working? She gets scared by loud noises—especially the sound of gates slamming closed."

Ty smiled and nodded. Jodi thought she heard him say "There's my girl," as he walked down the stairs.

Jodi made her way downstairs. She took a few bites of toast, washed the dishes in the sink, then she sat at the kitchen table. *I was sitting here when Ken first called about Solomon . . . ugh. Why couldn't God have made a mute button for the human mind?*

She walked across the kitchen and sat down in front of her computer. She needed to let the HopeWell volunteers know about Solomon—along with those families who had worked closely with him. *Should I call? What do I say?* Knowing she would never be able to get through that many phone calls, Jodi shook off the idea. Deciding a text would be more personal than an email, Jodi composed a message and sent it to each individual she knew would be most affected by Solomon's death. When she returned to the HopeWell office tomorrow, she would send out an email to their larger base of supporters and share the news on their social media sites.

A few minutes after sending the first of ten texts, her phone began dinging with messages of heartbreak and condolences. The third reply was from Shawn's mother, who expressed her condolences and asked if they were going to do anything to honor Solomon's life. She also said Shawn would be devastated by the news. Jodi knew the feeling.

"We will definitely plan something," Jodi typed back. "I

want to give everyone the opportunity to say goodbye. Please tell Shawn how much Solomon loved being his friend."

Feeling emotionally and physically drained after replying to several more texts, Jodi made herself a sandwich, then went to lie down on the sofa. Two hours later she awakened with a stiff neck. As she sat rubbing at one of the knots in her shoulder, a barrage of questions raced through her mind. *What impact would Solomon's death have on sessions? What about little Michael, who had just started bonding with the horse? What about kids on the autism spectrum?* Solomon had always had an innate ability to work with them. What if they couldn't find another horse with his same sensitivity and understanding?

Now, feeling anything but tired, Jodi stood, laced up her shoes, and headed out the back door. Her mind was racing with all the possible ramifications from Solomon's death—and soon her feet were racing too. She made a complete loop around the house. Then she walked around and through their vegetable garden—pausing to pull a few weeds and water some wilting herbs. Still feeling on edge, she walked to the bunny barn, but even the fluffy little bunnies couldn't ease the tension in her heart and mind. Her phone buzzed in her back pocket with a message from Ty.

Had to run back to the hardware store. Trip #3! Be back soon.

Jodi glanced at her watch. How had it gotten so late? Ty had been working on the fence all day. Several bleats and nickers reminded her that it was getting close to feeding time. "I can't put this off forever." Jodi walked to the feed shed and began mixing the grain, oats, and supplements each horse needed. She dreaded laying out the bowls and having to take Solomon's away. But once all the bowls were lined up, she realized Solomon's wasn't there. She looked around the ten-by-ten area. Moments later, she spotted Solomon's bowl, lying on a low shelf—a handful of black-eyed Susans arranged inside.

Ty.

Touched by his thoughtfulness, Jodi gathered the flowers in her hand and touched their petals to her face.

"I miss you," she whispered. Putting the flowers back in Solomon's bowl, she added, "I hope you're getting to eat all of your favorite things right now."

Jodi closed her eyes—and gave free rein to her imagination. She pictured Solomon in heaven, eating his fill of carrots and apples, oats and peppermints, and then taking off in a full gallop across a lush green field. When a little girl with blonde pigtails and brown cowboy boots appeared on his back, Jodi's hands flew to her heart. *Hope!* Jodi wished the beautiful image could stay in the forefront of her mind forever.

Gathering all the bowls in the wheelbarrow, she decided to feed Mercy first. After all, she told herself, the round pen was closer to the feed shed.

"Hi, Mercy," Jodi called. "Are you hungry?"

The dark bay horse looked toward Jodi, then turned her head away.

"I'll just leave your bowl right here. You get it whenever you're ready."

Jodi slid the black rubber bowl under the round pen fence. "I get it, you know," she spoke softly. "I'm not quite ready to do a lot of things either. I'm definitely not ready to go over there yet." The sound of something banging against a metal gate caused both Jodi and Mercy's heads to turn toward the sound. "But I guess Bubba Jack is telling me that, ready or not, he would like his dinner."

Mercy took several steps toward her bowl.

"I agree, girl," Jodi said, putting her hands on the wheelbarrow handles. "We can do this."

Jodi slowly pushed the wheelbarrow forward. It got heavier with every step. Forcing her head up, she looked toward the herd—all lined up awaiting dinner. In the front was Victory, back in the space he had occupied until Solomon had proved himself a more capable leader. The old quarter horse had resumed his leadership role in the herd. And Jodi knew he would keep it until his death—or until a younger horse proved as worthy as Solomon. Jodi squared her shoulders and took a deep breath before placing Victory's bowl in front of him.

"Here you go, big guy," she said, patting his neck as he lowered it.

She went down the line, giving each horse their respective bowl and a loving touch. When the wheelbarrow was empty, she went back to get their hay. She retraced her steps, leaving hay in boxes and bags and picking up the bowls. Yet when she went to retrieve Bubba Jack's bowl—which for some reason he insisted on moving around their pasture—a disturbing image flashed in her mind. As she pictured Solomon's body lying in the middle of the field, it slowly morphed into an image of her baby girl's lifeless body in her arms.

The images hit like a one-two punch to her heart. She wrapped her arms around her midsection. "No," she commanded herself. "NO!" Jodi squeezed her eyes shut. She counted to ten. She focused on her breathing. *In through the nose. Hold it. Out through the lips.*

An equine exhale behind her caused Jodi to spin around. Lady was standing behind her. The black-and-white horse, with her sweet and sassy temperament, usually brought a smile to Jodi's face. But today, Lady's presence highlighted Solomon's absence. A fierce anger rose up inside of Jodi. Her hands began to shake, her insides quivered. Pressure was building in her lungs. She ran toward the gate, the dreams and plans she had made for both Solomon and Hope taunting and mocking her.

Jodi ran from the field, past the hitching post where Solomon had gotten so scared, and was approaching the feed shed, when a pain in her side brought her to a sudden stop. She bent at the waist and rubbed at the cramp as her tears fell to the ground. Jodi's breaths came in short pants as grief, loss, and fear threatened to choke her. *It's too much*, Jodi's heart screamed. *I can't do this . . .*

Surrender.

Like the night before, she felt the word, more than heard it. And like the night before, she responded with incredulity.

"Surrender? I thought I was supposed to fight! Fight *and* surrender? That doesn't even make sense!" Jodi cried.

Anyone walking by would think she had lost it completely. She didn't care.

"God, I can't do this again. I need your help. If you are there, please help me!"

The moment the exasperated words left her lips, the storm inside of her ceased raging. The stillness in her soul was so jarring that she gasped. She knew that this feeling—the unexplained and unexpected stillness—could only come from God. The author of peace was whispering to her soul. And even though she didn't understand what he was saying, she had spent enough time with him over the years to know she could trust him.

"Lord, I *have* surrendered!" she protested. Jodi straightened her back and found the cramp had lessened. Standing to her full height, she gave full vent to her frustration. "I laid down my mask. I've been real with people. So real that I'm standing in the middle of a ranch talking to a God I can't see! What else do I have to surrender? Haven't you taken enough?"

Surrender, my child. Lay it down.

Jodi's knees buckled. She knelt in the cool grass. "I have, Lord," she sighed. "I've laid down the mask. I've laid down my plans—my dreams. But it still hurts so much." Jodi buried her face in her hands. "And it feels so . . . dark." Jodi looked up at the cloudless sky. "God, if it's really your voice I'm hearing—and not some grief-induced hallucination—help me understand what you want from me. I don't understand."

Jodi slowly rose to her feet. Exhausted and empty, she wanted nothing more than a hot bath and some chocolate. But she remembered the empty bowls and wheelbarrow. As she stood between the hitching post and feed shed, trying to will herself to go back and get them, she felt someone's gaze on her. She looked to her left. Two almond-shaped black eyes were focused on her.

Jodi walked toward Mercy. Her heart swelled with compassion for the lonely-looking mare. As Jodi got within six feet of the round pen, Mercy turned and moved to the opposite side. She stood with her body parallel to the fence. Her ears up, her muscles tensed.

"You've been through so much, and now this. I am so sorry. You are safe now."

Feeling a need to prove her words to the horse, Jodi carefully opened the gate and walked into the round pen. Mercy's head rose, her wide eyes tracking Jodi's every movement. But Jodi did not walk toward her. Instead, she walked slowly and purposefully opposite of Mercy and turned away from the pony. Jodi inhaled deeply and exhaled forcefully. The sound brought a sad smile to her face as she remembered all the breaths she had shared with Solomon. She could only hope that one day Mercy would feel as safe and secure as Solomon had. Jodi forced herself to relax. She wanted to communicate through her posture that there was nothing she expected from Mercy. She simply wanted to be present with her. To stand with her as she healed. As she learned to trust again. As she laid down her pain.

Lay down your pain.

Jodi's breath caught in her throat as understanding rushed in like a flood. *I've laid down my mask. I've surrendered the future I thought I would have. But I've been holding on to the pain, haven't I? Guarding it as if it's the only connection I still have to Hope.*

"God, is that true?" she whispered, knowing with certainty it was. Laying down the pain of losing Hope felt like having to let go of her all over again. And yet, an intense feeling of determination swelled inside of her—like a tide of truth rushing over her heart. Truth she needed to speak aloud.

"My grief isn't what connects me to Hope. God, you do. I believe she is with you right now. And I believe you are with me." A wide smile erupted on Jodi's face. "Oh, Father . . . help me to lay down the things that aren't mine to carry, so that I can hold tight to the things that are. Help me to fight the darkness by surrendering to your light."

Jodi knew these words held the power to heal her weary heart. She continued to pray, thanking God for his overwhelming love and for meeting her in the middle of a manure-covered pasture. As she stood breathing in the peace only he could offer, something bumped Jodi's shoulder.

Mercy.

Jodi was startled, but she didn't react.

"Well, hello, Mercy."

Jodi wanted nothing more than to throw her arms around the horse and celebrate what felt like a huge breakthrough for them both, but she remained still. Jodi silently pleaded for Mercy to surrender. *Lay down your pain, sweet girl. We don't have to carry it anymore.* Jodi's heart felt light and free, even as her legs started to cramp. But she would stand here as long as it took for Mercy to understand that she meant her no harm.

Moments later a velvety muzzle lay against Jodi's shoulder. Mercy exhaled forcefully. The beautiful, hard-fought exhale of surrender. Jodi reached behind her head and gently rubbed Mercy's neck and chin. The horse exhaled again. The weight of her chin pressed against Jodi's shoulder.

"There you go, love."

Jodi spoke aloud the very words God was whispering to her soul. Woman and horse stood together for several minutes. Holding on to each other as they let go of pain. And yet, even as Jodi laid it down, she knew that she would inevitably try to pick it back up from time to time. Just as she knew that while Mercy had made a huge breakthrough, she would still default to patterns of fear. Jodi vowed to help Mercy build trust and confidence in her. At the same time, Jodi felt an invitation from God to grow her trust in him.

"Lord, I trust you," she spoke aloud. "Help me to trust you more."

Much to Jodi's surprise, Mercy's fuzzy lips began rooting around her collar, nibbling at the fabric. Jodi chuckled softly and turned to face the mare. She expected Mercy to step away. She was pleasantly surprised when she did not.

"Sorry, girl, no treats in there. But I promise to bring you some tomorrow."

Mercy's pliable lips moved to the ends of Jodi's hair. Coarse whiskers tickled her neck. Jodi marveled at the transformation happening before her eyes—the horse who had been avoiding her now clamored for her attention. Jodi tentatively reached her hand toward Mercy's head. When she didn't flinch or turn away, Jodi ran a finger down the white stripe on Mercy's muzzle.

21

"I MISS SOLOMON," Shawn told Jodi a week after the horse's death. "I want him to come back."

"Oh, Shawn, I do too," Jodi replied. She longed to ease the boy's pain, but experience had taught her that the road to healing must pass through the valley of pain and loss. Jodi held up a small flat stone. "Would you like to make something for Solomon?"

She directed Shawn's attention to the art stations she and several HopeWell volunteers had set up earlier that morning. After receiving countless messages of support and shared grief over Solomon's death, the team had decided to host a celebration of Solomon's life. Tables had been put around the ranch, each one serving as a place where people were invited to honor Solomon or simply process their grief in a tangible way. There was a table with paper, pencils, pens, markers, and paint; one with photos of Solomon, blank scrapbook pages, stickers, and embellishments; and one with flat stones, paint pens, acrylic paint, and brushes. By providing a variety of materials, Jodi hoped that those wishing to grieve through their hands would have the materials to do so. And for those who wanted to talk through their grief, Jodi, Linda, Tania, and Amanda were available to listen. Visitors were invited to sit with the bunnies, visit the goats, and interact with several of the horses who were stationed with volunteers at various hitching posts. So far the weather had cooperated, and, in spite of the heaviness of loss, everyone seemed to be enjoying the day.

"Can I paint two rocks?" Shawn asked. "I want to give one to Solomon, and I want to keep one."

"I think that is a wonderful idea, Shawn."

Jodi scanned the crowd. Several small children were running near the bunny enclosure. All of the art stations were full. Linda was talking with Shontell and two other girls. Tania was introducing a crowd of children to Opie. And Amanda was talking with several parents of kids currently in their program. Jodi turned her head to check on the herd, her gaze automatically going to the middle of the field where Solomon's body had been. Would that image ever be erased from her memory?

As her focus broadened, Jodi noticed Mercy running back and forth along the back fence line. The young mare was undoubtedly feeling anxious with all the activity around her. Jodi managed to catch Linda's attention. She pointed to herself and then to the field and held up five fingers. She and Linda had worked together long enough that the older woman nodded her understanding that Jodi was taking five minutes to check on Mercy.

As thankful as Jodi was for all the people who had come out to celebrate Solomon's life—and as much as she loved being able to honor the horse in such a beautiful way—she was grateful for a few minutes by herself. She welcomed the quiet and allowed it to fill her like fuel she would need to get through the rest of the afternoon. The moment Mercy spotted Jodi, she ran to meet her. It was hard to believe that just a week ago the pony would have run *away* from Jodi. Mercy's eagerness warmed Jodi's heart, even though she suspected the horse's excitement had more to do with the treat she hoped was in Jodi's pocket than with Jodi herself.

"Hi, sweet girl," Jodi called out as she approached the fence line. "Feeling a little nervous, huh?"

Mercy hung her head over the fence, near enough to claim her prize. Her lips parted and moved in opposite directions. Jodi chuckled as Mercy's upper lip curved around the beige cube in Jodi's open hand. She made fast work of chewing the treat and extended her head for more.

"Don't get too excited. I only brought two with me."

Gleeful children's voices drifted from the center of the ranch. Jodi closed her eyes and prayed—for Shawn, for Mercy, and for everyone at HopeWell. As she was thanking God, once again, for all he had done through Solomon's five years at the ranch, a loud sound caused her to jump. The noise brought a fearful whinny from Mercy. Someone must have tipped over a folding chair. She turned her attention to the distressed mare.

"This will be over soon," she soothed. "I promise things will quiet down." She bent down, ripped out a handful of tall grass, and offered it to Mercy.

"A little stress eating always helped Solomon calm down."

Jodi took her time walking back to the main area. But as she approached the pavilion, she saw someone whose presence caused her to pick up the pace.

"Michael!" Jodi called out with a wave. "I am so glad you came today."

"Hi, Ms. Jodi!" he said, wrapping his arms around her waist. "I'm really sorry about Solomon. He was a nice horse."

"Thank you, Michael. And I know for a fact that Solomon thought you were a really nice boy."

"My dad said that a wild animal attacked him. Is that right?"

Jodi hesitated for a moment. Her instinct was to hide the details from Michael. Children shouldn't have to deal with such things. Yet she knew that most of the children they worked with at HopeWell had experienced things far worse than the death of an animal. In fact, many had dealt with more pain and loss than most of the adults Jodi knew. As Jodi looked into Michael's trusting eyes, she realized that any attempt to hide the truth or evade his question would keep his questions in the dark—where fear casts long shadows. She reminded herself that what Michael needed—what everyone needs—is a safe place to talk about hard things; and to invite God to shine his light onto the dark shadows.

She put her hand on his shoulder. "We think a wild dog got into the field and tried to hurt Solomon and the other horses."

"I bet Solomon was really scared."

"I'm sure he was," Jodi answered, the reality of that statement causing her throat to constrict. "In fact, we think he got so scared that he ran through the fence and galloped for a long time."

"Do you think he was chasing the mean animal away?"

Jodi shook her head slightly. "I don't think so. Horses usually run away from danger—especially from other animals that might try to hurt them. But what do you think that wild dog would have thought about a thousand-pound horse running as fast as he could?"

Michael's eyes grew wide. "That dog would have been so scared. He probably ran away like a scaredy cat!"

"I think you are exactly right, Michael," Jodi replied. "In fact, I bet Solomon scared him so much he will never come back here." Michael nodded vigorously in agreement.

Wanting to give Michael a little more information, Jodi continued. "After running as fast as he could, Solomon's heart and lungs started to have trouble working—his lungs had been sick for a while. We think Solomon must have been very tired and went back to his field to rest. Once he was back inside—and made sure his friends were safe—we think that Solomon's heart and lungs got so sick that they stopped and he died."

Jodi paused to allow time for Michael to absorb her words. His ocean-blue eyes looked into hers as if searching for something.

"Solomon was very brave," the young boy announced.

"He was very brave indeed," Jodi agreed.

Michael abruptly turned away from Jodi and called out, "Hey, Dad!"

Michael's dad is here? Jodi had assumed he'd come with his mother or that his dad had stayed in the car. "Dad!" Michael called again, as his father slowly walked toward him. "Solomon was brave—just like you! He ran back to protect his friends. Just like you did."

Michael pulled Chad's arm toward Jodi. "This is Ms. Jodi, remember? She taught me how to ride Solomon."

Chad gently pulled his arm from Michael's grip and extended his hand to Jodi.

"It's nice to see you again, Jodi. Mikey really wanted to come today."

"Daaaad!" Michael whined.

"Sorry, bud. I meant *Michael* wanted to come," Chad corrected with a wink. "I can't get used to your big guy name."

Jodi chuckled. "It's so nice to see you again too. I'm so glad you both are here."

Jodi wanted to thank Chad for his service, but anything she thought of sounded trite. *How do you even begin to thank someone for dedicating their life to protect and defend others?*

"Ms. Jodi, can I go paint one of the rocks?" Michael asked.

"Absolutely, Michael."

"Make sure you follow the instructions and behave yourself, Michael."

"Yes, sir."

"You have a great kid," Jodi said, turning back to Chad.

"Thanks. He really is pretty great." He looked down at the ground. "Hey, um . . . thanks for being there for my boy. I imagine he's told you about . . . well, that it's been a bit rough these past months." Chad cleared his throat. "Anyway, I just wanted to, you know, say thanks for giving Mikey a place to be a regular kid."

Chad raised his eyes to look at Jodi. "And, um, I'm real sorry about your horse. That's tough."

Jodi sensed that his admission had not come easily. She received his words as a valuable gift.

"Thank you, Chad." She hoped he could see the sincerity in her eyes. "And thank you so much for your service."

"Oh yeah . . . sure thing," Chad answered, shoving his hands in his pockets.

Chad took a step back. His eyes darted around the ranch. Instant regret—and confusion—washed over Jodi. *Did I say something wrong? Was it wrong to thank him? Why did I have to say anything at all?* Wanting to undo whatever damage she may have done, Jodi began to ramble.

"So . . . well, we have lots of different activities going on today. Ways for people to share memories of Solomon. Or to say goodbye. Or to thank him for . . ." *Ugh, why did I have to bring up the whole* thank you *thing again?* Jodi mentally chided herself and then rapidly moved on. "People can visit the bunny barn. Bunnies are actually really good at helping people feel calm. Oh, and our goats are over there." Jodi pointed toward the goat enclosure, but her words kept flowing. "We are so thankful for the beautiful weather. Our horses are too. They love this weather—and the extra attention. Well, all except for our newest horse, that is. She's not at all happy about today's events." Jodi's gaze flew to Chad. She didn't want him to think she wasn't grateful for everyone attending today's event. "I mean, *of course*, we're so happy to have everyone here. So thankful that everyone came out to honor Solomon. It really is a beautiful day, isn't it?"

Dear heavens! Jodi paused long enough to take a breath and ask God to open the ground and swallow her whole. *Could I sound more ridiculous? The weather? Did I really just talk about the weather?*

"Why isn't the new horse happy?" Chad asked, interrupting Jodi's tailspin.

"Well, our newest horse was recently rescued from a bad situation, and she bears a lot of scars—most of which you can't see. But they run pretty deep. And since we really haven't had a chance yet to get her used to the sounds of the ranch on a busy day like this, it's causing her a lot of stress."

Jodi paused for a moment as an image of Solomon flashed in her mind. "Solomon actually had a calming effect on her. I think he had appointed himself as her protector." Jodi cleared her throat. "I think today might be extra hard for her without him here."

Chad's attention shifted to the pasture.

"Which one is she?" he asked.

Jodi pointed to the dark bay mare with the white stripe standing by herself at the far end of the field. Chad nodded and rocked back on his heels, then turned his attention toward the table where Michael was painting a stone. Then he looked toward the parking lot. He reminded Jodi of a skittish horse. Wanting to throw him a lifeline, Jodi invited him on an impromptu tour of the ranch.

"Only if you have time," she added, giving him an out.

"Ms. Jodi!" Shontell ran to Jodi. "I miss Solomon so much. I'm so sad he died."

Jodi held the girl close. "I am too, sweetheart. He was a very good horse. And you were a very good friend to him. Thank you for loving him so well."

Shontell squeezed Jodi tightly. "He was a good friend to me, too. And he was super easy to love. Will you come to his grave with me? I want to put my rock on it."

"Of course I will. Just let me . . ."

She turned to Chad to ask if they could start their tour in fifteen minutes, but he was gone. Would she ever get another chance to speak with him? Assuming he had gone back to the car, Jodi decided she would walk Michael to the parking lot when he was ready to go.

Twenty minutes after Shontell had placed her stone—painted sky-blue with the letters *BFF* written in chestnut brown—at the spot where Solomon was buried, Jodi returned to the pavilion. Richard, Jessica, and her boyfriend, James, had arrived. Jodi embraced them and thanked them for coming. Many past and present volunteers offered their condolences, each one also sharing a memory they had of Solomon. Doctor Pol, his wife, Diane, and their son, Charles, along with Dr. Brenda and several crew members from the television show, also came by to offer their support. Jodi was so touched by the outpouring of love from the HopeWell community that she felt true happiness for the first time all week.

"Thank you so much for being here," Jodi said to the small crowd gathered in the pavilion. "And not just today, but every day—the good days and the hard days. You all have made this ranch into a real community. You've turned it into a family. A family who can celebrate together and grieve together."

Heads nodded in agreement as she concluded her impromptu speech. Many hugs were given, and a few tears were shed. As the crowd began to disperse, Michael tugged on the back of Jodi's shirt.

"Do you know where my dad is? I want to show him the rock I made for Solomon. But I can't find him."

Jodi swallowed hard as she read the word *hero* painted in red letters against a blue and white background. Jodi put her arm around the boy as she scanned the crowd. Not seeing Chad, she started walking Michael toward the parking lot. After realizing where they were headed, Michael came to a stop.

"I already checked the car. He's not there."

Now Jodi was getting concerned. *Where could Chad have gone? He wouldn't leave his son, would he?* Jodi spotted Ty near the office. She started heading that way with Michael, when movement along the side of the pasture caught her eye. Was it the wild dog returning? Jodi stopped abruptly. Her grip tightened around Michael's shoulder. Michael looked from Jodi toward the field.

"Oh! There he is!" Michael said, taking off in a carefree run.

Jodi felt as if someone had punched her in the stomach. When her breathing returned to normal, she was able to see clearly what her fear had obstructed before: Chad standing across from Mercy.

"Dad, look at the rock I painted for Solomon!" Michael was saying as Jodi joined the pair.

"That looks real good, Mikey."

Michael grinned from ear to ear. "I was going to put it where he's buried, but—" Michael cast a hopeful look at Jodi—"I kind of want to keep it. Is that alright?"

"Of course. In fact, I think that is a great idea."

"Which horse is this one?" Michael asked, pointing at the pony standing across from him.

Jodi answered Michael but looked at Chad. "This is Mercy. She's our newest horse—well, actually she's a pony. And she's been a little scared today."

Jodi paused as Michael observed Mercy. "But how does she look to you now, Michael?"

Michael studied Mercy. He leaned forward slightly and pursed his lips, concentrating deeply. "She looks pretty happy, I think. Her back foot is bent up. Her ears are up, and her head is down. That means she's happy, right?"

"It sure does, Michael. Mercy looks happy and content right now. I'm so glad your dad was able to stay with her while we had our goodbye party for Solomon. I think he helped Mercy feel safe."

Michael patted his dad on the back. "Good job, Dad!"

"She probably just needed to know she wasn't all alone out here, that's all," Chad replied. He ruffled Michael's hair. "Sometimes that's all somebody needs to know."

22

"I CAN'T BELIEVE HOW MUCH this garden has grown in three months," Amanda said, walking into Hope Garden. "It's beautiful in here."

Jodi shielded her eyes against the morning sun as she greeted Amanda. She rose from her seat in the dirt and took in the garden she had been tending all summer. Glossy, dark-green viburnum bushes, yellow-green buttonbush, and blue-green blueberry bushes were adding depth and fullness to the rectangular space. Black-eyed Susans, crimson butterfly-weed, and cheery yellow daisies added subtle pops of color. Jodi still had a long way to go before the garden resembled the inviting wonderland of her imagination. But as she thought back to the bare dirt Ty had presented her several months earlier, the transformation was pretty spectacular. But even more meaningful to Jodi was the way the garden helped her feel connected to

Hope—and even to Solomon, since she had a tendency to talk to the plants as she watered and pruned them.

"This garden has been such a gift," Jodi said, brushing the dirt from her jeans. She noticed the papers Amanda was holding. "But I take it your visit has more to do with the paperwork in your hands than with the plants in the ground."

"Guilty as charged, but I think people are really going to be grateful for this memory garden."

Jodi had first mentioned the idea of a memory garden at their last staff meeting. She had described it as a place where others could sit and remember loved ones they had lost. A safe place where they could grieve, or even have the opportunity to add to the garden in memory of their loved ones. The team had loved the idea, and the decision was made to open it to the HopeWell community the following spring.

Jodi looked forward to inviting others to add their own personal touches to the garden, but she wanted to establish a good foundation first. Happy with the progress she had made this morning, Jodi stood up and reviewed the day's schedule in her mind. They had a school group due to arrive in an hour for a tour; a group of at-risk kids coming in the early afternoon; and sessions scheduled into the evening. It was time to put away her spade and pruning shears and get a halter and lead line.

Hours later, Jodi stood in the arena with Linda, watching Michael lead Mercy around the perimeter.

"Good job, Mikey!" Chad called out from his position at the gate.

Jodi still couldn't get over how comfortable Chad seemed at the ranch these days. The week after Solomon's celebration of life event, Chad had walked Michael to his session and casually asked about Mercy. The next week he had brought a carrot for Mercy. At Michael's next session, Chad had asked to stand in the pasture with Mercy while Michael worked with Samson. Last week, Jodi had asked Chad if he and Michael would be willing to help with Mercy's training.

"I've been working with Mercy for several weeks now," Jodi had explained, "and she's doing great. But I think she's getting a little bored with me and Linda. We could really use your help."

After Jodi explained the process of desensitization, Chad and Michael had enthusiastically agreed to help. The four of them spent the hour introducing Mercy to squeaky toys, plastic bags, and orange cones. At first Mercy had been on high alert, but as she became more familiar with her surroundings, and the people with her, she had started to calm down. At the end of their hour, Chad and Michael had asked if they could work with Mercy again the following week.

Now, as Jodi stood in the arena watching father and son, she suspected Chad was getting as much out of his time at HopeWell as Michael and Mercy were. Leaving Michael in Linda's capable care, she walked over to the gate.

"He's doing a great job," Jodi said, motioning to Michael. "He seems to have a gift for putting Mercy at ease."

"Yeah, he does seem to have a gift for that," Chad answered, pride evident in his voice. But his next words were full of regret and sorrow. "I guess it's probably because he's had so much practice."

"You don't sound too happy about that."

Chad shifted his weight to lean against the gate. "I just mean that . . ." Chad paused, as if deciding what to say. "I just hate that he feels like he has to work so hard to keep me from having an episode."

During Michael's previous sessions, Jodi had learned that Chad referred to his PTSD symptoms as episodes—with some episodes being far more intense than others. Jodi kept her gaze on Michael and Mercy as Chad continued.

"I mean, I've been doing a lot better. I've even started seeing a shrink at the VA. But Mikey . . . he still feels like he has to walk on eggshells around me. I mean, he's a kid. He should be able to be loud and do stupid stuff without worrying that he's gonna cause his old man to lose it, you know?"

The muscles in Chad's arms twitched as he spoke. A vein bulged in his forehead. Jodi wished she could ease his pain and concern. She wished she felt more equipped to help him. But as she watched him watch Michael, she reminded herself that while he had experienced things she never would, he was also just a concerned parent, worried about his son. And so Jodi did what she would do for any parent who stepped on the HopeWell grounds—and what she had received herself from others at the ranch. She listened. She was present. And she provided space for him to share or remain quiet.

"You care a great deal about Michael."

"That I do," Chad replied with a sad smile. "He's a great kid—so much better than I was at his age. And he's put up with a lot. It's been great to see him out here. The first time I saw him running around out here, I felt like I saw a glimpse of the boy he was before my last deployment. Before everything seemed to change. It was almost as though the last eighteen months had never happened."

Chad grew quiet as Linda spoke to Michael in the middle of the arena. Mercy stood contentedly at Michael's side.

"Did I tell you what happened that first night, the night after I met Mercy?" Chad asked, his attention still focused on his son.

"No."

"I slept." A burst of laughter reverberated through Chad's chest. "I mean, I hadn't slept more than two hours at a time in . . . well, probably in years. Between deployments and nightmares and insomnia, let's just say the whole eight-hours-a-night thing has been pretty tough. Brutal, actually. But that first day I came out here and you told me Mercy's story? I don't know what it was, but I just got it, you know? Like I got her. I felt like I *was* her."

Chad kept his eyes on Michael but continued to speak to Jodi. "Anyway, while I stood out by the pasture that day, I just kept telling her that she was safe now. That she had a home and good people to help her. And I don't know . . . it was like that night as I was lying in bed, I kept hearing my own words in my head. That probably sounds crazy or something. But as I listened to my own words, I started to get tired. Next thing I knew, the sun was up and I had slept for nine hours. Nine hours! I apparently freaked my wife out because she said she kept checking to make sure I was still breathing."

Jodi inhaled deeply. "Oh, Chad, I don't even know what to say. Praise God. That's wonderful!"

Chad chuckled again. "God? Mercy? Fresh air? Probably a combination of all three. I don't know what it was, but something happened—which I guess explains why I've kept coming back here. I forgot how much I like to sleep," he added with a sheepish grin.

Jodi didn't know if she wanted to sob or shout for joy, but her indecision was cut short when Michael called Chad and Jodi over.

"Hey, watch what Mercy can do!" he shouted.

As Chad and Jodi approached, Michael held his arm in front of his face and began to wave it back and forth. Mercy took two steps back.

"She can back up!" Michael said, his face beaming.

"Well done, Michael," Jodi praised.

"Good job, Mikey," Chad said simultaneously.

"Can I walk her around the arena one last time?"

Jodi readily agreed, delighting in the confidence she saw radiating from Michael as he led Mercy. When Michael reached the gate where Jodi and Chad had been standing, he stepped on a wayward squeaky toy. Mercy's head pulled against the lead line. She let out a half-hearted whinny. Michael froze and dropped her line.

"I'm sorry!"

Jodi and Chad hurried to him. Mercy didn't move.

"What happened, Michael?"

"I . . . I didn't see the toy. I didn't mean to scare her."

Chad squeezed his son's shoulder, then patted Mercy's back. "I think she's stronger than she was, Mikey. Look at her."

Michael nodded, his eyes shining. Jodi agreed with Chad's assessment and encouraged Michael to finish walking Mercy.

As Jodi and Linda waved goodbye to father and son at the end of their session, Jodi turned to Linda.

"I want to serve veterans," Jodi blurted out.

"Serve them what?" Linda asked, breaking into a grin. "Sorry," she chuckled. "I know what you mean. And after witnessing the transformation in Chad the past few weeks, I'm all in. But what about the whole 'we don't have experience with military life' thing? You wanted to do this before but then didn't. You sure about this?"

"I am 100 percent sure," Jodi declared.

"What changed?"

"I realized that I'm stronger than I was. And it's time to start acting like it."

23

A MONTH AFTER DECLARING HER INTENTION to offer some kind of program for veterans, Jodi and Linda attended the annual Equine Assisted Growth and Learning Association (EAGALA) conference. At previous conferences, they had enjoyed a variety of breakout sessions about all the different programs related to the EAGALA model. But this year, they signed up for the military track—where their sole focus would be on learning as much as possible about how to best serve veterans and their families.

The first session included an army chaplain who shared about the importance of understanding military lingo. He covered the different branches of the military, their particular strengths, and how they are organized. Jodi took copious notes as the chaplain spoke. At the end, he took questions from the attendees.

"You stated that the VA is looking into a variety of alternative mental health services. Why are they thinking this is necessary?" a woman inquired.

Jodi dug through her purse for a new pen.

"I once heard an army captain state they can teach you how to be a soldier," the chaplain began, "but they can't teach you how to be a civilian again. This is what makes things so difficult for our veterans when they re-enter civilian life. They know how to relate to other veterans, but they have a very hard time becoming who they were before enlisting."

Jodi scribbled notes as fast as she could, but given how quickly the man talked, she was wishing she had brought a voice recorder.

His cadence picked up as he kept talking. "And since most families expect to welcome back the same person who left, there is a lot of pressure on a veteran to pretend to be that same person. Deployment can mean different things for our men and women. Some see horrific things, experience great loss, and suffer from personal or moral injury, and returning to a 'normal' civilian life can feel jarring and disorienting. And not always in the ways you might think."

Setting aside her notes, Jodi leaned forward in her seat, absorbed by the amount of valuable information. "For instance, when a wife is worried about what type of dress to wear to a party, her veteran husband may look at her with disdain as he thinks about the men he lost to an IED—and how trite a party seems in comparison. He will likely begin to feel as if he can't understand her needs any more than she can understand his. Or, in the case of parents, there's often great difficulty for veterans trying to reengage in day-to-day parenting decisions—as well as for the spouse, who has functioned as a single parent for an extended amount of time and now has to partner with someone again. New roles have to be established, and that can be incredibly difficult for someone dealing with trauma and the stress of re-entering civilian life."

He paused to take a sip from his water bottle. "Of course, those are just two examples of how the stress of daily life can weigh on a veteran. Those examples don't even come close to addressing the weight of survivor's guilt, the toll of physical pain, or the hopelessness of emotional pain. Our veterans are struggling. And with statistics revealing that there are fifteen to twenty *documented* suicides per day among veterans, they clearly need more help than the VA can provide. That is why offering these types of services—like equine therapy, for example—is so vital. How about we take a break, then reconvene in fifteen minutes?"

As Jodi and Linda walked to the refreshment table, Jodi was silent.

"How are you doing?" Linda asked.

"A bit overwhelmed. Twenty documented suicides per day! That can't possibly be true. Can it? Oh, Linda, I can't even imagine . . ."

"So what are you thinking, Jodi?"

"I'm thinking we have to do something. *Now.* We need to pull together a group of veterans who would be willing to assist us in creating a program and getting it off the ground as soon as possible!" Her resolve strengthened with every word.

"I'm in," Linda agreed.

Jodi and Linda spent the remainder of the weekend learning as much as they could about the needs veterans had—what issues troubled them the most; the importance of understanding that post-traumatic stress is something that happens *to* them and not *who* they are; how secondary PTSD can affect caregivers; and how the hands-on team approach of the EAGALA model can effectively help serve veterans struggling with a variety of issues.

Jodi left the conference feeling as though a fire had been lit inside of her. It was a drive—a determination—she hadn't felt in years, not since she pounded fence posts in the ground all those years ago. She knew she was meant to start a program for veterans. And she knew exactly who to ask to help get it up and running.

U

"Why do I feel so nervous?" Jodi asked Linda, as they stood in the pavilion waiting for their guests to arrive.

"Because this matters to you. Because this matters, period," she clarified.

Jodi nodded. Getting their veterans program started mattered a great deal. She looked at the trees throughout the ranch. Most of them had already lost their leaves, but a few hardy stragglers remained—tiny crimson, orange, and yellow flags waving against a deep blue sky. Jodi pulled the zipper higher on her jacket as the autumn wind kicked up.

"I'm glad we're doing this today. It seems like winter is trying to bully its way in."

The day after Jodi and Linda had returned home from the EAGALA conference, just over two months ago, they had begun working on a curriculum and format for their veterans program. Jodi mentioned the idea to Chad at her next session with Michael. Chad had said he thought it was a great idea. But when Jodi asked him to consider serving on a board of advisors, he grew quiet. His muscles tensed, and he took several steps back.

Realizing she had put him on the spot, Jodi tried to back-pedal. "Please don't feel like you have to, Chad. I just really respect your opinion and value your input. And I just thought that maybe . . . I mean, you certainly don't have to . . ." Why did she get so tongue-tied in situations like this?

"Why don't you just think about it and get back to me whenever you'd like?"

Jodi turned her attention back to Michael and Mercy as they worked with Linda in the arena. She asked God to give her wisdom to know how to proceed, especially if Chad didn't want to be a part of the program. She was just about to join Linda inside the arena when Chad cleared his throat.

"You sure you want *me* to be involved with this?" he asked, with eyes full of vulnerability.

"Absolutely," Jodi assured him. "In fact, I can't imagine doing this *without* you—without your guidance, advice, and input. We want to do this well, Chad. Really well. We want it to be helpful to veterans and their families. And we've been asking God to provide us with people to help us accomplish that. We really believe one of those people is you."

Chad pressed his lips together. He nodded several times. He opened his mouth. Closed it. Then opened it again.

"Thank you, Jodi," he finally said. "For everything."

Now here they were, waiting to welcome their first veterans

to the ranch. Chad had agreed and was bringing a friend. As two cars pulled into the parking lot, Linda announced, "I do believe our beta-testers have arrived."

Hit by a sudden case of nerves, Jodi hesitated. "What if this doesn't go well? What if Chad's friend doesn't get it? What if we end up doing more harm than good? What if . . ."

Linda put her hands on Jodi's shoulders and looked her in the eye. "And what if this program ends up helping people? What if veterans, and their loved ones, find healing out here? What if you are doing exactly what you were put on this earth to do?"

Jodi rested on Linda's words. The weight of what they wanted to accomplish with the veterans program had been weighing heavily on her all day. She wiped her eyes and shook her head.

"You're right," Jodi said. "We've prayed about this. We've researched and prepared. We've listened and learned. And now all we can do is give it our best try. Thank you, Linda. And thank you for suggesting this trial-run."

Linda thought a trial-run would provide valuable feedback so they could work out any kinks before incorporating the veterans program into their spring session planning for next year. Jodi had loved the idea and had immediately called Chad to ask if he would be their first participant. There was a slight hesitation, and Jodi had feared he was going to say no. But Chad had simply asked if he could bring a friend—a fellow veteran—with him.

"That way I won't be the only guinea pig!"

Jodi had eagerly agreed and made arrangements for Chad and his friend Jerry to come by the following week. Now, as Jodi watched Chad and Jerry slowly approach the pavilion—both with their hands in their pockets and their heads down—she had the distinct feeling they were second-guessing their offer to help.

"Thank you both so much for coming out this afternoon," Jodi said after introductions were made. "It really means a lot to us that you're willing to help us. We want this program to be helpful and meaningful for our veterans. And we will gladly welcome any feedback you are willing to give us."

Both men nodded. Jerry, an older man who was tall and thin with a beard that rivaled the Robertsons on *Duck Dynasty*, thanked Jodi for allowing him to come out to the ranch.

"I haven't been around horses in a long, long time. Actually, I can't even remember the last time I was up close to one."

"Well, we can certainly fix that," Jodi said with a smile.

As they walked across the ranch, Jerry and Chad listened as Jodi and Linda briefly explained their vision for the veterans program—to provide a peaceful, therapeutic environment where veterans, current servicemen and women, and their families can experience healing through interaction with horses. Then Jodi shared their goals for the night's run-through, which included helping them identify any issues or potential problems before opening the program to the public. The men nodded their understanding, and the group set off for the large field.

"How exactly does this horse therapy stuff work?" Jerry asked as they walked. "I think I rode a horse once as a kid. But it sure didn't change my life or anything. And it sure didn't cure me from being a pain in the . . ." He gave Jodi a sheepish look.

Jodi offered him a warm smile. While she appreciated his effort to watch his language, she wanted him, and all of the veterans they would serve, to feel comfortable expressing themselves in whatever way they needed to—as long as it didn't hurt anyone else. She made a mental note to talk to Linda about how to incorporate that into the introductory talk they would give at the beginning of the military sessions program.

"Jerry, I like to think of what we do here as less like therapy and more like building relationships that can help us heal and grow. Riding is a part of that—it has its place, just like taking a walk with a friend does. But it's not the focus of our program."

She stopped beside a hitching post. "HopeWell is all about providing opportunities for people to relate to another living creature. In many cases, it's easier for someone to bond with an animal, like a horse, than with another human—especially if they've been hurt by people in the past. Oftentimes, it can feel safer and easier to open up to an animal than to another person. And horses, in particular, have a unique ability to work with people because of how they relate to us."

"What do you mean?"

Jodi appreciated Jerry's curiosity. "Well, horses can act like mirrors to us—*if* we're willing to pay attention to what they reveal. For example, if I'm working with a horse and I'm tense—maybe on edge because of something that happened that day—the horse I'm working with will become tense. Or if I'm fearful, the horse will likely assume there is something to fear. If I enter their space feeling angry and distracted, my horse is going to become difficult to work with. If you want to know how you are really feeling about something, go spend some one-on-one time with a horse. If you let them—if you learn to slow down and pay attention when you're with them—horses can reveal things to you about yourself. Things that can help you find peace and point your heart toward healing."

Jerry looked skeptical, yet his eyes held a glimmer of hope. Jodi hadn't planned to say anything about Solomon, but she felt an overwhelming urge to do so now.

"I actually experienced that peace and healing myself out here several years ago when I was working with one of our horses. His name was Solomon." A twinge of grief poked her heart as she said his name. "He helped me realize that I was hiding my feelings behind a mask. That I wasn't being real with the people I love and trust. By working with him, I eventually realized that the mask I was wearing had grown too heavy and was keeping me from experiencing joy and honesty in my relationships."

Jerry let out a chuff of disbelief. "Why in the world would someone like *you* feel like you had to wear a mask? What would a good woman like you need to hide?"

His words felt more like an accusation than a question, but Jodi saw them for what they were—an opening. She could feel Chad and Linda staring at her, but she kept her focus on Jerry.

"I think all of us, at least at some point in our lives, try to hide behind a mask, Jerry. For me it was a mask of pretending to be okay when in reality my heart was breaking from grief. For others, though, it might be a mask of strength when they feel weak, or a mask of indifference when they feel too much."

Jerry was quiet for a few moments. A horse whinnying in the distance caught his attention.

"You're the second person this week who said something to me about wearing a mask." He sounded more annoyed than angry. He picked at his thumbnail and spit to the side. "But I'll tell you what I told him—ain't nobody want to see what's underneath that mask. I guarantee you that!"

Jerry's eyes narrowed. Jodi knew she needed to proceed carefully.

"Part of what we hope to do with our veterans program is provide a safe place for people to be who they are—underneath the masks, outside of any expectations. We want to walk alongside you as you pursue the goals you set for yourself." Jerry was silent, but his eyes remained fixed on Jodi's. "I wonder if maybe one of your goals might be to explore who you are underneath the mask you wear."

Jodi expected more silence. What she got was an explosion.

"Are you kidding me! You think anybody wants to see the monster that lives inside of here?" he shouted, pounding his chest. "You think anybody wants to hear about the things I've seen. The things I've *done*? Shoot, they'd run screaming as far away from me as they could get. And let's just say I wouldn't blame them. Not one bit."

Jerry's breath was coming in pants. His face was red. His eyes were wide, and he seemed to be focused on some haunting image only he could see. Jodi worked hard to keep the shock from her face. Chad put his hand on the back of Jerry's neck and squeezed.

"You're okay, man," Jodi heard Chad say. "Just breathe."

The men lowered their heads, and Jodi could hear Chad's voice but couldn't make out what he was saying. Of all the things she had expected for this trial-run, this moment was not one of them. As swiftly as a flash flood, doubt and insecurity threatened Jodi's resolve. *What made you think you were qualified to work with veterans? Tonight proves that you have no business creating this program. Just apologize for wasting their time and send them home.* Yet, somewhere in the middle of her mental assault, the whisper of a promise broke through. A promise she had been reminded of earlier that morning as she read from the forty-first chapter of Isaiah. She quoted verse thirteen to herself, "I am the LORD your God who takes hold of your right hand and says to you, Do not fear; I will help you" (NIV). Jodi closed her right hand and asked God to let his words of truth become a shield against the taunts and lies being hurled at her.

Her fear demanded she quit.

God's love persuaded her to walk on.

Jodi looked up. She was surprised to find Linda standing beside her.

"You did good," Linda spoke softly. "He is exactly where he needs to be."

Jodi's heart grabbed hold of Linda's words. "Okay," she whispered.

A moment later Jerry lifted apologetic eyes to her. "I'm sorry, ma'am. I didn't mean to blow up like that." He rubbed at his forehead. "I just . . . I mean, I . . ."

"Jerry," Jodi said, taking a step toward him, "you are in a safe place. And we want you to be free to express how you are really feeling." She shook her head slightly and gave a self-deprecating laugh. "And trust me, I've blown up a lot worse than that out here." Jerry and Chad's eyes widened. Jodi laughed in earnest. "That's actually another reason why I prefer to talk to horses when I'm really stressed. They don't spill the beans to anyone else when you cry and scream and let it all out!"

Moments later the group followed Jodi through the gate. Several equine heads turned in their direction.

Jodi extended her arm toward the herd. "Gentlemen, meet the horses of HopeWell."

She briefly introduced the horses—pointing to each one, giving their name, and a brief description of how they came to HopeWell. Jodi then invited the men to walk around and introduce themselves to the herd. Both men looked at her skeptically, but they set off in search of a horse.

Chad stopped and visited with Samson, Beau, and Bubba Jack before making his way to Mercy. Meanwhile, Jerry hesitantly approached Justice, then casually made his way to Opie, and finally came to a stop near Victory. Jodi and Linda walked to the water trough to give the men space to be present with the horses they had chosen. Jerry was standing awkwardly beside Victory, with his feet slightly apart and his hands interlocked behind his back—a soldier standing at ease. But his expression was more reminiscent of someone awaiting a root canal.

Victory gave Jerry a cursory sniff, then slowly walked away, leaving the man standing alone in the field. Deciding it was time to intervene, Jodi started to move but then slowed her pace. Lady was approaching Jerry from the right. Seemingly startled by Lady's approach, Jerry took several steps to his left. Lady stopped to study the stranger in her field.

Jodi suppressed a chuckle as horse and man stood facing each other with their heads tilted to the side. Jerry took a tentative step forward. Lady didn't move. Jerry moved closer. Lady stretched her head forward. Soon he was standing inches away from the black-and-white pinto. Jerry cautiously stretched out his hand and allowed Lady to breathe in his scent. Lady nudged his hand with her nose, then rubbed her muzzle against the bottom of his long beard. Jerry's laugh rang out across the field. Linda gave Jodi a thumbs-up.

Twenty minutes after first entering the field, Jodi invited

Chad and Jerry to lead their horses to her and Linda. Chad had done a similar exercise before, so he began to walk toward the women. But Jerry was looking around.

"Don't I need a leash or something?" he called out.

Jodi shook her head. "Nope, you have all you need. Just start walking and invite Lady to follow."

Jerry looked from Jodi to Lady and back again; he took several steps, paused, and turned back to Lady, who hadn't moved an inch. Jodi chuckled softly as Jerry walked back to the horse, bowed at the waist, and swept his right arm toward Jodi and Linda. "Madam . . ."

"It's like *Duck Dynasty* meets *Downton Abbey*," Linda whispered, forcing Jodi to bite her cheek to keep from laughing.

When Lady didn't accept his invitation, Jerry repeated the motion. When she still didn't move, he looked to Jodi and shrugged.

"Why don't you just start walking over here and let's see what happens," Jodi called out.

Jerry glanced at Lady, then started walking toward Jodi. He held his hands up apologetically.

"Guess she didn't care to accept my invitation," he said as he got closer. "Probably needed a leash after all."

Jerry stopped when he noticed Chad approaching from his left with Mercy following dutifully behind. A look of sadness—or maybe rejection—flashed across Jerry's face as he watched the pair.

"You're gonna have to teach me how to get these things to follow me," Jerry said with a bitter laugh.

"I think you managed just fine on your own there, dude," Chad chuckled, nodding his head beyond Jerry's shoulder.

"Well, I'll be . . . ," Jerry said, turning and finding Lady a few feet behind him. He reached out and ran his hand along Lady's shoulder. "What do you know."

His bemused expression tugged at Jodi's heart. She and Linda joined the men and their horses near the front of the pasture. They chatted about the horses they had met and why they had chosen the ones they did.

"You know I have a thing for Mercy," Chad said. "I was just trying to be polite to the others until I could get over to her."

When it was Jerry's turn to share, he looked as uncomfortable as he had been standing beside Victory. "I just stopped beside that one horse because I got tired of wandering around trying not to step in horse poop. But then that horse left." Jerry spoke the words as if Victory's leaving had been a foregone conclusion. An awkward silence fell over the group. Lady bumped Jerry's arm with her muzzle, eliciting a laugh from the man. "But then this pretty thing walked up to me and, well, she followed me over here!"

As Jerry reached out to stroke Lady's long neck, his befuddled expression pricked Jodi's heart.

"You seemed a little surprised to find Lady behind you," Linda observed.

"I sure was!" Jerry admitted. "Only way I used to get my dog to follow me was if I had a piece of meat in my hand."

Jerry studied Lady as if she held a mysterious secret he wanted to discover.

"Why do you suppose she followed you, Jerry?" Linda prodded gently.

Jerry continued to study Lady. "Lord if I know," he mumbled.

He never took his eyes from the horse. "Hope it ain't 'cause I smell like the back end of one of her friends."

The group laughed with him, but Linda was undeterred by his attempt at redirection.

"What do you think Lady sees when she looks at you, Jerry?" she asked.

Jerry stared at Lady's feet before raising tired, weary eyes to Linda.

He tugged at his beard. "I guess . . . well, I suppose she sees a tired, beat-up old man with a horse's tail on his face!"

While the image he described brought another laugh from the group, his words felt like an invitation—one Jodi had every intention of accepting. But first, Jodi showed the men how to halter their horses so they could lead them to the arena. Once inside the covered building, she demonstrated how to use the currycomb to loosen debris and dirt from their horses' coats. As they brushed, she talked about how grooming not only helps to keep the horses clean and healthy, but how it also helps to build trust between horse and human.

"Basic grooming will be a part of each session we do with our servicemen and women—just like it is with all of our sessions. It's a wonderful way to build trust with your horse," Jodi said.

Linda then explained that they would normally have some sort of an activity or assignment after grooming their horses. "We might ask you to build an obstacle course for your horse or complete a task together. Or lead them from one area to another without using a lead line," she added with a wink.

Jodi handed each man a soft brush and showed them how to run it over the horses' coats in short strokes to flick off any remaining dirt or dust.

"You might need one of these for that tail on your face," Chad teased.

Lady let out a noise that sounded a lot like a sigh.

"Feels good to get rid of all that dirt, doesn't it, girl?" Jerry asked. "I bet that junk feels awful heavy on your nice coat."

As the men resumed brushing, Chad asked Jerry about his knee. Jodi was able to infer that Jerry had sustained a knee injury while in Vietnam that still caused him pain. She also learned it was during a round of physical therapy that he met Chad at the VA hospital. Jerry answered Chad's question, and then their conversation turned to the various injuries they had suffered, the frustrations they faced living with chronic pain, and the difficult time they had sharing their pain with well-meaning family and friends. Eventually, their conversation turned toward invisible wounds and scars—and the ways they tried to manage them.

"Drinking helped until it didn't," Jerry said as he brushed the soft hair below Lady's mane. "It was the only thing that turned it off, you know?" Chad nodded. The pain in his eyes told Jodi that he understood more than she possibly could. "I just wanted to stop thinkin', stop feelin'. I just wanted to be numb. Lived that way for decades. I mean, feelin' numb felt better than feelin' broken, you know?"

"Oh man, I know," Chad replied.

"Anyway," Jerry continued, "one night, a while back, I took off from the bar—numb as could be—with my buddy in the passenger seat and ran my car right into a tree. We got banged up real bad. But it was a bloody miracle we didn't get killed— or that I didn't kill somebody else. Lost my license for a bit, did the whole court thing. But I just kept thinking about how

I could've really hurt someone. I didn't want that. I felt like enough of a monster as it was!" Jerry spit over his shoulder.

"I didn't want to feel anything anymore and thought about taking my own life. But soon after plowin' into that tree, I decided to give it up. I'm two years, six months, and twenty-seven days sober."

Jodi, Linda, and Chad erupted into applause. "Man," Jerry said, looking at the ground, "I ain't told nobody that story for a long time."

Jodi looked at both men. "Seems like you both have been carrying some pretty heavy things for a really long time."

"I suppose we have," Jerry said.

"Do you ever wish you could lay it down, even if just for a minute?" Jodi asked.

The men looked at each other briefly, then back at Jodi, and nodded.

"*That's* what we want HopeWell to be for you. We want this to be a safe place to lay down your pain. And the masks you feel like you have to wear—and any expectations you feel. Even if just for an hour." Jodi motioned to the horses standing at rest behind the men. "And these special horses want to help carry some of that load. After all, they were created to carry heavy loads."

"Not the load of garbage I drag around."

Linda took a step forward. "Jerry, would you tell us a little bit about the kind of garbage you carry around?"

Jerry motioned to Chad with his head. "He knows what I'm talking about."

Chad nodded.

"That junk will mess with you. The stuff we saw, the things

we—" he cleared his throat—"the things we had to do just to stay alive. Let's just say, it changes the person you see staring back at you in the mirror."

Jerry and Chad shared a little about the horrors they had witnessed in combat; the friends they had lost; and the substances they had used to numb their pain. Jerry also spoke of returning home from Vietnam and feeling like the country hated him for what he had done. "I felt like a monster over there, only to come home and find out most people over here agreed that I was."

Gratitude and heartbreak swirled in Jodi's heart. She felt honored that the veterans were willing to be so transparent, but she also wanted to weep for all they had endured. Yet this was not about her—not about her discomfort or pain. She would not give them a reason to try to shield her from their reality. She would weep later as she prayed for them. But in this moment, she would simply be present and listen.

As Jerry was talking about his last deployment, Jodi noticed Mercy lower her head. A few minutes later her front legs bent and her knees touched the ground—immediately followed by her back legs. As if demonstrating with her body the act of laying down one's burden, Mercy lay down behind Chad. He looked from the horse to Jodi, his eyes asking if Mercy was okay. Jodi smiled and nodded.

When Jerry finished, Jodi had to fight to keep her mouth from falling open as Lady followed Mercy's example and lay down behind Jerry, letting out a loud exhale as she did. Unable to contain the joy pulsating through her heart, Jodi directed the men's attention to the resting horses behind them.

"Guys, what do you think Mercy and Lady are telling you right now?"

"That they've got our back," Chad eventually said, his voice tight.

"That if it's too hard to reach up and put our junk on them . . ." Jerry's gruff voice broke. He cleared his throat and continued, "that they'll come down here to get it."

Whoa. Jodi hadn't been prepared for that answer. Thankfully, Linda spoke up, agreeing with Chad and Jerry, before diving a little deeper into the gift of helping hold one another's burdens. As Linda grew quiet, Jodi spoke up.

"May I tell you what I see?" she asked.

The men nodded.

"I see two horses telling their new friends that they like who they see. And who they see is who you *really* are, because horses can't see the masks we try to wear. They only see what *is*. These two horses see you, and they are choosing to stay right here—with you."

Jodi thought she had been unprepared for Jerry's answer, but it was nothing compared to his weeping. Feeling a familiar urging deep within her heart, Jodi moved closer.

"Jerry," she said softly, placing her hand on his shoulder. "The way those horses see you is an imperfect reflection of the way God sees you. The fact is, the God who made these beautiful animals incapable of seeing masks is the same God who looks at you and sees you for who you are. He sees your heart, not a mask. Not a broken or tired man. Not even your tail of a beard," she teased. "He sees you. Jerry. His child. Made in his image. And loved beyond your ability to comprehend. Whatever you are feeling from Lady is but a fraction of what God wants to give you."

Jerry bowed his head as another wave of sobs made his shoulders, hands, and beard shake. The horses never moved.

Thirty minutes after Chad and Jerry left, Linda and Jodi sat in the HopeWell office. Both women were emotionally and physically exhausted, and yet they were too excited and exhilarated to go home.

"I was not expecting that," Jodi admitted. "I was thinking we'd go through the motions of a veteran's session, not actually have one—and certainly not one like that!"

"Me either," Linda agreed. "But if we ever doubted whether or not we needed to do this, I believe we just got our answer."

A comfortable silence settled over the room, each woman lost in her own thoughts. After several minutes, Linda said, "What are we going to call this program? We haven't given it a name yet."

A name was definitely important, especially now that there was no doubt they would be starting the pilot program in the spring. They certainly couldn't call it the "Equine Therapy for Veteran and Active Military Service Men and Women, and Their Families" program!

Jodi closed her eyes as the image of Jerry weeping in the arena drifted into her mind. She had been so moved by his tears. Perhaps because they had reminded her of her own tears. Tears she had shed as God worked through Solomon to help her lay down the mask she hadn't even known she was wearing.

Solomon. Sweet, sweet Solomon . . .

"Solomon!" Jodi blurted out, startling Linda. "What if we name it after Solomon?" Jodi jumped up. "Think about it. He helped me lay down the mask I was wearing. *And* he was a strong, steady leader who loved his herd." The next words caught in Jodi's throat. "Who gave his life to protect his herd."

A single tear trickled down Linda's cheek as she nodded in agreement.

Jodi closed her eyes as a flood of memories washed over her. "I once told Solomon that I felt like I was his special project, like he was sent just for me. But the truth was, he made an impact on many people."

Jodi's eyes widened. Her index finger shot up.

"Project Solomon! What if we call it Project Solomon?"

"Project Solomon," Linda repeated. She smiled, said the name again, then rose to her feet. "It's perfect."

"Well, okay then. We've got a name, and we've got a format. Now we just need some veterans!"

24

IT'S HARD TO BELIEVE that Project Solomon was just an idea two years ago, Jodi thought as she filled the last of the water troughs, enjoying the feel of the cold water on the warm June day. Of course it was also hard to believe that within that same time period she had gained a son-in-law, James, and—if her mother's intuition was correct—she would soon be gaining a daughter-in-law, Rebekah, as well. Jodi adored James and Rebekah and had gladly welcomed both of them into their family—a family she hoped would soon include lots of grandchildren that she and Ty could dote on.

As the water reached the top of the trough, she turned off the spigot. Her leg muscles ached as she walked the short distance, a reminder it had been an active and busy day. They had hosted a team-building event for faculty at Mid Michigan College; Dr. Pol and his family made a surprise appearance to drop off a donation; and the HopeWell staff was making sure everything was ready for tomorrow's barbecue fundraiser for Project Solomon. Jodi barely had time to sit down.

So much had happened, it was hard to remember what life had been like before HopeWell. People were reporting significant improvements in the issues that had brought them to the ranch as they participated in general sessions or Project Solomon. Jodi was grateful to be part of the beautiful tapestry God had been weaving all along.

Jodi was starting to wind up the hose when her phone buzzed. Jerry was calling.

"Hi, Jerry. How are you today?"

Jerry didn't call often, but when he did, it was usually because he or a friend was having a hard day. During his time in the Project Solomon program, Jerry and Jodi had developed a code to help him on his hard days. Jodi would ask how he was, and if he answered with "How's Lady?" Jodi would text him a picture of Lady. The picture served as a reminder that he was not alone, that he was seen and loved, and that his life mattered. Jodi had texted him quite a few photos over the last two years.

"I'm okay. But I wanted to see if I could bring a buddy of mine over to visit the horses for a bit? He's having a pretty hard day."

Jodi had learned that Jerry was the king of understatements, so she knew in her gut that his friend must be in a very dark place.

"Of course, Jerry. Is there anything I can do?"

There was a moment of silence on the other end before Jerry answered.

"Maybe say a prayer for him. Russ—my buddy's name is Russell—we served together a long time ago. Anyway, I heard from another buddy that Russ wasn't doing so good. So I decided to stop by and check on him. He didn't look good. Said there's no point in going on. Too much pain for too long. Said he's done. I recognized that look in his eyes."

Jerry cleared his throat. "I told Russ to get himself dressed 'cause I was taking him to a place where he can find some peace." Jerry paused again, then continued with a tenseness in his voice. "And then . . . well, I said the dumbest thing I've probably ever said. I told him that if he still wanted to do what he was planning to do after he spent time out here, I wouldn't try and stop him."

Jodi's heart skipped a beat. *Oh, Lord . . .*

"I know I shouldn't have said it, but Ms. Jodi, I knew he wouldn't come out here if I didn't say it. And I had to do something. Russ has been through a lot over the years. He's been dealt some bad cards. The man just needs . . . I just want him to find what I found at HopeWell."

After ending the call, Jodi fell to her knees beside the spigot and prayed for Russ and Jerry and for all the men and women who were staring darkness in the face at that very moment. "Oh, God," she prayed aloud, "shine the light of your mercy and grace into the darkness. Wrap your arms of love around these lonely and hurting individuals. Envelop them in your peace. Whisper your name to their hearts. And let them see a way out—let them glimpse you."

Jodi continued to pray as she finished her chores. Jerry had said Russ lived an hour away, so by the time all the animals were fed, and things were put away, Jodi expected to see a car pull up. She debated whether or not she should greet them. Since Project Solomon began, Jodi had learned a great deal about giving veterans time and space to grieve and process their pain. But she had also learned that they can often feel alone, unseen, and unloved. And so she decided that while Jerry could certainly introduce his friend to the herd, she would greet them and let them know how honored she was by their visit.

As the sunlight filtered through the tops of the tall pines flanking the western border of the ranch, Jodi sat in the pavilion and waited for the men to arrive. When she heard two cars pull up, she started walking in their direction. Jerry was walking beside a man who could easily pass for Santa Claus. But as the men got closer and Jodi could see Russ's eyes, she realized there was no jolly twinkle there. Only emptiness and pain.

"Jerry, it is so nice to see you. I'm so glad you both were able to come out today."

"Thanks for having us, Ms. Jodi," he said, then nodded toward his friend. "This here's my buddy, Russ. I told him you got a great place out here. Could we go over and visit Lady for a bit?"

"Absolutely. Hi, Russ. I'm glad you came out today," Jodi said, extending her hand. Russ shook her hand, made brief eye contact, then averted his eyes.

"Lady will be thrilled to see you, Jerry." The two had formed quite a bond. Jerry credited Lady with giving him a reason to wake up each day. After eight weeks in the program, Jodi had noticed a lightness to Jerry's demeanor. She had mentioned her observation to him. He had simply shrugged and said, "I guess it's because I don't have to wear a mask out here. Lady accepts me—the good, the bad, and the really ugly. And since I haven't scared you all off yet, I'm guessing that means the rest of you do too."

Jodi hoped that someday Jerry would fully believe that God accepted him like that too.

"You guys make yourselves at home. I have some paperwork to catch up on, so I'll be in the office if you need anything."

Jerry tipped his baseball cap to Jodi. "I'm going to grab some brushes from the tack room, and then Russ and I will head to the pasture." As they walked off, Jodi heard Jerry teasing Russ. "That mane of white hair you have could use a horse brush too!"

A few minutes later, she saw the two men talking beside Lady, near where Solomon had lain. Yes, God can bring life from the ashes of death. HopeWell had been born from loss. Project Solomon had been born from loss. Both were now being used to bring life.

Life born from death.

Freedom found in surrender.

Community formed out of loneliness.

Jodi peeked out the window before sitting at her desk. Jerry was showing Russ how to move the brush in long strokes down Mercy's back.

Mercy.

Of all the horses out there, of course Mercy would be the one to join the impromptu session. "Thank you, Lord."

An hour and a half later, Jodi sat back in her chair and rubbed her eyes. Her paperwork pile was gone, and so was the sun. She stood up and stretched. She was grateful to have gotten a lot of work done, but she was disappointed she had missed saying goodbye to Jerry and Russ.

As Jodi stepped out of the office, the sky had turned a deep indigo and it was cooler than when she had greeted them. Ty had called an hour earlier to check on her. She had filled him in on Jerry's impromptu visit and explained that she was catching up in the office while the two men spent time with the horses. "I'll be home soon to help with dinner," she told him.

But when she looked toward the pasture, she saw two figures. She strained her eyes to get a better look. *Jerry and Russ? I can't believe they are still here.* The two were standing at the gate when she approached, and she could hear Jerry talking about Mercy.

" . . . been through a lot . . . basically on her own. Owner didn't do a thing to take care of them. The horses were out there every day starving. Doin' what they could just to survive. Mercy's even got the scars to prove it. Got scars on her gums and tongue and the front of her legs from where she would rip tree bark to eat."

Russ spit out a curse as Jerry continued. "She's been through hell, man. And I don't know half as much 'bout horses as Ms. Jodi does, but I bet Mercy came over here 'cause she senses that you've been there, too, you know?"

Not wanting to intrude, Jodi remained in the shadows outside the gate.

"Being out here can help, man," Jerry continued as Russ rubbed his sleeve across his face. "Just brushing 'em like we were doing can help. It . . ." Jerry struggled to find the right word. "It slows everything down a little bit, you know? Gives you something to focus on. Sometimes when I brush Lady, I try to match my breaths to hers. Or to the brush strokes. I don't know . . . that probably sounds weird."

Russ shook his head. "Nah, I get it."

Jerry spotted Jodi. He nodded in her direction, and she gave a little wave. Then he gave her an unspoken invitation to join them.

"Did I tell you 'bout the first time I met Lady? How she laid down at the end of our time?"

Russ shook his head and laughed. "You bored her that bad?"

Jerry's beard danced as he chuckled. "Ha! I couldn't bore a sloth, you know that! Nah, we'd been talkin' about the masks that we wear. The ones we try to hide behind, trying to pretend we ain't the monsters we fear we are." Russ nodded.

"Well, after talking about that stuff for a bit, Lady laid right down behind me. It was like she was saying, 'Man, put that thing down. You don't need it here. Just lay it down like this.' And you know what? She was right. Ms. Jodi says horses can't see masks. They can only see who we really are. Like Mercy here. She sees the real you. And look! She's still here, ain't she?"

"Yes, she is," Russ said, looking at Mercy gratefully.

"Ms. Jodi says that God is like that too. That he don't care a lick about masks. And that he's right here too. And you know what? I'm startin' to think she may be right."

Jodi had to keep from gasping at Jerry's last statement.

"Your mask has just gotten too heavy, man, that's all," Jerry said, his eyes focused on Russ. "But it's okay, 'cause you don't need it anyway."

Russ cleared his throat when he noticed Jodi. He gave her a sheepish smile.

"Sorry we've been here so long."

"Oh no," Jodi interjected. "Please don't be. I am thrilled you're still here. And so are Mercy and Lady. I was worried I had missed you. I just came by to say goodnight."

Jerry and Russ thanked Jodi for letting them come out. "Jerry was right. This is a cool place. I feel better than when I got here." Then Russ paused, took a deep breath, and added, "In fact, um, Jerry says you guys have some kind of program for veterans. Maybe I could join?"

"You would be a great addition to our veteran family, Russ. I'll get your number from Jerry and send you all the information."

"Yeah, that'd be great. But would I be able to . . ." He looked at Mercy.

"Yes. Mercy will be a great horse for you to work with when you come out," Jodi said.

"That'd be good." He patted Mercy's back. "That'd be real good."

25

Jodi gently pressed a handful of sunflower seedlings into the soil. She had always loved the cheerful-looking flowers and knew they would make a wonderful addition to Hope Garden.

"It's hard to believe these tiny seedlings will grow to be ten feet tall in a few short months," Jodi said to Jessica as the two of them placed the tiny plants throughout the garden.

Jodi stopped and looked at her daughter. Tears of joy once again filled her eyes. She rose and hugged Jessica for the tenth time since her daughter and son-in-law, James, had shared their news. Jodi and Ty had been delighted when Jessica had suggested a Father's Day picnic out at the farm. Since Richard had to work on Sunday, they had decided to have the picnic the day before—and had even offered to help her and Ty in the garden.

Jodi couldn't have imagined a more perfect day . . . until Jessica handed Ty a gift bag containing a framed ultrasound photo. Jodi had jumped up and run to her daughter as soon as she saw the gift, while Ty had remained seated, joy pooling in his eyes. "A baby . . . ," Jodi had reverently whispered, placing her hand on her daughter's abdomen. "Oh, thank you, Lord," she had prayed aloud. "Protect Jessica, protect this precious little baby. Let this little one grow healthy and strong. Oh, God, thank you for this gift of life."

Now, a few hours later as mother and daughter stood in the garden—the garden created as a tribute to Hope—Jodi felt like she could spend the rest of her life thanking him, and it still wouldn't come close to being enough. But she would try.

Taking her daughter's hands in hers, she said, "But the change in these small plants is nothing compared to what is happening inside of you right now. You're going to be a mommy! And I'm going to be a grandma!"

After finishing with the seedlings and adding a few more flowering bushes to the perimeter of the garden, Jodi and Jessica stood back to admire their work.

"Can you see it, Jess?" Jodi asked.

Jessica looked questioningly at her mother. "See what? The sunflowers?"

Jodi smiled. "Can you see the beauty that will soon overwhelm this garden? The sunflowers that will stretch toward their Creator. The flowers that will welcome butterflies, bees, and hummingbirds to a lavish feast." Jodi turned and placed her hand on Jessica's belly. "Can you see your child picking flowers? Making mud pies? Chasing bunny rabbits? Holding up an earthworm for you to admire?"

Although Jessica cringed at the last image, joy radiated from her face.

"How do you do that, Mom?" she asked, her voice full of wonder.

Jodi was so caught up in the images of her future grandchildren playing in Hope Garden that it took a moment for her to register Jessica's question.

"How do I do what?"

"See things others can't? Like seeing beauty—and family—where others just see dirt."

At first, Jessica's words made Jodi laugh. But as she thought about them, her heart swelled with gratitude.

"I think too many times in my life I tried to see things with these eyes," she said, pointing to her own, "but all I could see was loss and darkness. But the day I pounded those very first posts into the ground—the day HopeWell was born—God invited me to see through his eyes. And it changed everything. It was just a glimpse—like peering through a blurry window. But it was enough. And now, it's the only way I want to see things."

"Is this a private moment, or can anyone join?" Ty said, as he, James, and Richard entered the garden.

"Did you leave any dirt for the plants?" Jodi teased, taking in her husband's dirt-covered shoes and gloves.

"That'll be enough out of you," Ty shot back. "We got the job done—we now have a sturdy, well-built picket fence that runs all the way around your garden. How we got it done doesn't matter. Right, fellas?"

Some movement near the large pasture caught Richard's attention. "Who's that over there?"

"Those are the men and women of Project Solomon," Jodi said proudly. "Their session was rained out earlier this week, so they asked if they could come out today. Not for formal sessions, but just to be with the horses. They said being with the horses helps them feel grounded."

Ty put his arm around Jodi's shoulders. "You gave them a family, you know. And a place to belong." He looked at the hand-painted sign Jodi had made for the entrance to the garden—Hope Garden. "Our little girl sure made a big impact here, didn't she?"

Jodi leaned her head on Ty's shoulder. "She sure did."

Ty pointed to the group of veterans. "That handsome stud of yours left quite a legacy too. Project Solomon is going to do a lot of good for a lot of people."

"I agree," Jodi said, taking in the scene in front of her— veterans choosing life; her family expanding with new life. Light breaking through darkness. The fulfillment of a promise God had whispered to a grieving heart so many years ago. The kindness and faithfulness of God felt like a tidal wave of grace.

"I can see it, Ty. I can see the lives that will be changed—the lives that will be saved because of that program—and because of HopeWell. And I am so excited. But you seem to have forgotten something."

She turned to face Ty, her eyes twinkling. "He was a gelding."

Epilogue

Jodi trudged through the small pasture to put out fresh hay for the miniature horses. As if the pandemic hadn't been enough, central Michigan was dealing with the worst flooding they had seen in a century. And while HopeWell, for the most part, had been spared, the reports coming from the surrounding areas described devastating damage and property loss. They hadn't been able to offer their normal sessions schedule in months—and Jodi had no idea if and when they would be able to resume normal operations. Thankfully, she and Linda had been able to put together an online curriculum for those children and families who had access to the internet. And while Project Solomon had not been able to meet in a formal capacity, they were still able to provide a safe place for those who wanted to venture out during the pandemic to come spend time with the horses. In addition to all the shifts and changes, they were also having to move their annual fundraiser to an online auction. A familiar worry settled over Jodi. *Will we have enough funds? How long can we continue like this?*

Worries continued their assault. Did they have enough hay to tide them over if the effects of the flooding made it difficult to find more? What was happening to their most vulnerable children? How were the veterans coping with so much isolation? And, assuming life returned to some semblance of normalcy soon, how would they ever be able to raise enough money to build a second arena for the veterans?

Sharing an arena with excited, often loud children presented challenges for veterans with severe post-traumatic stress, and Jodi longed for them to have their own designated space. They had actually been planning to kick off a fundraiser to create a second arena right as the pandemic hit. *How will we ever manage to raise money for that now?* And then there were the increased calls from first-responders looking for support—wanting to know if they could join Project Solomon. Jodi's heart longed to say yes! But how could they possibly take on more clients now? *How are we supposed to make plans for the future when the present is unknown? Ty and I aren't getting any younger. Should we even be worrying about this at all?*

"Lord, what are we doing? And how are we going to keep doing it?" Jodi asked aloud as she pulled the gate open. "Please show me what to do. I just need a word from you."

In spite of her prayer, a feeling of despair and an overwhelming weariness settled over Jodi. As she exited the field, rain started to fall—again. Just then, her phone rang. *Jerry.* She dashed into the arena to escape the downpour.

"Hi, Ms. Jodi, I have my buddy Carl on the phone with me.

He and I spent some time with Mercy this morning—before the blasted rain started up again. Anyway, he wanted to speak with you. So I'm gonna put him on the phone now."

"Hi, Ms. Jodi, this here's Carl. I just wanted to say thank you."

There was a prolonged silence. Jodi feared that they had gotten disconnected. But then she heard Carl clear his throat.

"Well, you see . . . I was . . ." He cleared his throat again. "I was planning on . . . ending my life today." Jodi's heart sank. "But Jerry here made me promise to first go out to HopeWell and meet some of your horses. I met Mercy. She just walked right over to me like she knew I was coming. She let me brush her while I talked a bit with Jerry. I just wanted to tell you that for the first time in a long time I think there might be a reason I'm still here on this earth. And I think maybe I should spend some time figuring out what that reason might be. So, Ms. Jodi, I just wanted to say thanks for what you're doing. And make sure you know that what you're doing really matters. It matters a lot."

All Jodi managed to get out was "Thank you, Carl," before he passed the phone back to Jerry.

"Jerry, thank you. You have no idea . . ." She had to stop before she started crying.

"Aw, Ms. Jodi, you call me—you call any of us—anytime you need a reminder that what you all are doing matters. You keep shining that light. And remember what you told me once: God loves you; he sees you; and he is for you."

Jodi placed her phone back in her pocket. She pulled her hood up and stepped out into the rain. It was time to get to work.

Welcome to HopeWell

A journey in pictures

Jodi and Ty with HopeWell's very first horses: Promise and TJ.

One of HopeWell's first clients, sharing a moment with Glory.

Jodi and Ty, working together with a client.

Jodi preparing Miracle to begin a session during HopeWell's first year.

Jodi on Victory (aka Sir Lick-a-Lot). He was a rock star horse, and many children took their first-ever horseback ride on him.

Jodi and Ty with their kids, Jessica and Richard.

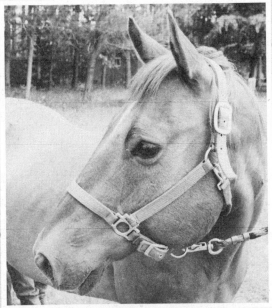

Solomon . . .
a "gentle giant" at heart.

Jodi riding Solomon.

Solomon with one of his favorite clients.

Solomon walking toward Jodi. His head-down posture communicates, "I trust you. You're part of my herd."

Solomon always makes Jodi and the client smile.

Siblings are often most comfortable riding together. Solomon loved children and was happy to walk with two on his back.

Solomon (middle) overcoming loneliness at last.

Making friends with the donkey Bubba Jack.

Jodi *(right)* and a volunteer preparing a client to ride Bubba Jack.

Samson and Jodi.

Doctors said Dakota would never walk or talk, but she proved them wrong. Here she is on Samson. She said her first-ever three-word sentence after riding him: "I did it!"

Lincoln receiving loving from HopeWell's Registered Student Organization at Central Michigan University.

Samson and Lightning, sharing breakfast.

Lessons in the Legacy Arena.

The herd getting to know a new member: Oliver (in the lead).

Raine dressed up by a client during
Project Aware, a program for at-risk students.

Opie and his herd-
mates during an
Eagala session.
When a horse rests,
there is always a
horse who will
stand watch.

Justice running in the round pen. He was
a mustang from Bald Mountain, Nevada,
who had a special relationship with many
veterans.

A Vietnam veteran walking with Justice.

Veterans doing a group obstacle course together.

Sierra walking with a veteran and a child.
A special moment showing what HopeWell
is all about.

Opie peeking out from behind a tree
in HopeWell's wooded pasture space.

A client who became especially close with Mercy. He bravely stepped up to try new things because he said, "Mercy is my courage."

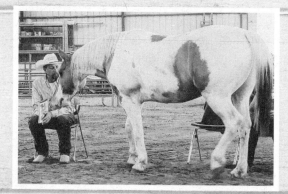

An instructor with Cody during an Eagala training.

Two veterans working with Lucy.

A volunteer and a client walking Blaze to a lesson.

The Three Kings:
Lincoln, Lightning,
and Blaze walking in
a winter wonderland.

Mercy in the snow.

Jodi and Ty with their family today.

The heart of HopeWell—Jodi, Ty, and Solomon, drawing
upon the love of Christ to move people toward healing.

In Appreciation for
Project Solomon

As a Vietnam veteran, I can say that HopeWell Ranch, along with their ministry of Project Solomon, continues to bring healing, help, and peace to veterans suffering with PTSD. Knowing Jodi's caring heart and the good that comes from equine therapy, I highly recommend this book.

TERRY, US ARMY AND GOLD STAR FAMILY MEMBER

My favorite part of being at HopeWell Ranch was the interaction with the beautiful horses and talking to my fellow veterans, as well as with the owners and all the workers there.

KATHY, US ARMY

Being in HopeWell Ranch's nonjudgmental and peaceful environment allows me to let go of my anxieties and be present in the moment.

BRIAN, US ARMY

The horses opened my eyes to methods that help me deal with my issues.

ROBERT, US NAVY

If it wasn't for Project Solomon, I wouldn't be here. The people at HopeWell Ranch are family to me.

JERRY, ARMY NATIONAL GUARD

Resources to Help Those
Who Are Struggling

If you, or someone you love, is struggling with feelings of hopelessness, thoughts of suicide, or symptoms of PTSD, the following organizations can offer help:

Suicide Prevention Hotline
(800) 273-8255

National Alliance of Mental Illness (NAMI)
(800) 950-6264 or email info@nami.org

American Psychological Association
https://www.apa.org/topics/crisis-hotlines

The following organizations offer help and resources for veterans, military, and first responders:

Veterans Crisis Line
(800) 273-8255 (press 1) or veteranscrisisline.net

Wounded Warrior Project
(888) 997-2586 or woundedwarriorproject.org

MindWise Innovations
https://screening.mentalhealthscreening.org/Military_NDSD

To learn more about equine therapy and the Eagala model utilized at HopeWell, as well as to find an Eagala certified therapy program near you, visit eagala.org.

Discussion Questions

1. *Project Solomon* opens with Jodi hammering fence posts into the ground because she feels called to do so. Have you ever felt called to take a step in faith to pursue a dream, even if you weren't sure how you would get there? What made you take that first step? What happened as a result?

2. What are some of the qualities Jodi notices about Solomon right away? Why do you think they stood out to her?

3. Jodi and Ty's children struggle with the demands of the ranch. Why do you think this is? Throughout the book, what does Jodi learn about balancing parenting with her calling to run HopeWell? Is there anything you would have done differently in her shoes?

4. What happens as Solomon gets to know his new herd? What parallels do you see between the way the horses respond to a newcomer and how people sometimes react in the same situation? Have you ever been the "outsider" trying to become part of a group? What was it like, and what did you learn in the process?

5. Which children connect most with Solomon, and what makes him so special to them? How does he help them process their own emotions? Why do you think these children feel so safe with him?

6. How has taking care of animals helped Jodi to heal from her own wounds throughout her life? In what ways have the animals brought comfort and healing? Has a beloved pet ever helped you or a loved one to process grief?

7. How do Solomon's and Jodi's transformations connect to one another?

8. Horses are herd animals that rely on one another to feel safe. Who are some members of your own "herd," and how do they help you to feel safe? In return, how do you do the same for them?

9. In chapter 9, we learn about the tragic event that caused Jodi to found HopeWell. How did founding the ranch help Jodi process her grief? What does the ranch's name mean to you in light of this revelation?

10. In chapter 11, a friend asks Jodi, "Why do you suppose you feel the need to hide your feelings behind a mask?" Can you relate? How would you answer that question?

11. In chapter 19, why does Dr. Brenda believe that Solomon returned to his herd when danger threatened? What does his sacrifice mean to Jodi? What happens at HopeWell as a result?

12. What does it mean to you that a human or an animal would lay down his or her life to protect the herd? What other examples of sacrificial love can you think of?

13. What was Solomon's relationship with Mercy like? How does she continue the work he began?

14. In chapter 23, Jerry has an emotional encounter with Lady. Why do you think he connected so strongly to her? What do you think Lady and Mercy were communicating by lying down as Jerry and Chad talked with Jodi and Linda?

15. Jerry said he wanted Russ to find the same thing he had found at HopeWell. What do you think Jerry found at the ranch? Have you ever invited someone to experience something that has profoundly impacted you? How did they respond?

16. In chapter 25, Jessica asks Jodi how she can see the potential of things that many others cannot see. Jodi says it's because she tries to look through God's eyes. What do you think she means? How does her perspective impact the ranch and those around her?

Acknowledgments

JODI STUBER

This book is first dedicated to my Lord and Savior, Jesus Christ, who knew that beyond my pain, healing and hope would come and resurrect my life into something I didn't know was possible.

To Ty, the love of my life, my favorite person who is a constant source of laughter and joy.

To Jessica and Richard, our amazing children, who have always been such precious gifts from God.

To James and Rebekah for seeing how "amazing" Jessica and Richard are and marrying them. You are the best son- and daughter-in-law on the face of the planet.

To our beautiful and precious grandchildren who spark delight in my heart every day. I pray you will always know you can do BIG things, even at a young age.

To my parents, who instilled in me a heart to work hard for what I believe in, serve those in need, and show compassion and love whenever I can.

To Jennifer Marshall Bleakley for coming into my life and

wanting to share the story of HopeWell Ranch with the world! Your incredible gift of writing through the lens of love has impacted so many people's hearts. Thank you for your beautiful words of life and hope.

To Sarah Atkinson and Bonne Steffen and Team Tyndale for your belief in this story and your incredible talents to make this book a reality.

To my wonderful team at HopeWell Ranch—the staff, the volunteers, and of course our incredible animals. HopeWell would not be what it is without you! I love you all very much! And thanks to everyone who participates in our programs. You have taught me how to be a better listener and a more compassionate person.

To Dr. Pol, Dr. Brenda, and the entire staff at Pol Veterinary Services in Weidman, Michigan, an extra special thank-you for the way you care for our animal crew. I am grateful for your expertise, thoroughness, and compassion, as well as your generous support of our ranch. Dr. Pol, thank you so much for endorsing this book. I am grateful for you and your friendship. I will always be one of your biggest fans.

Last but not least, I would like to thank our veterans and their families for the sacrifices they have made to keep our country free.

God has indeed blessed us.

JENNIFER MARSHALL BLEAKLEY

In October 2019, I was asked to speak at HopeWell's annual fall benefit. Happy to lend my support to a worthy cause, I gladly accepted. I was excited to speak about the powerful ways horses can help people find healing. And really, that was all I thought I would do during my visit. But as I stood with Jodi on a cool misty morning at her ranch and listened as she shared about the pain of loss that had birthed the HopeWell ministry—and about the veteran program named in honor of a horse who laid down his life for his herd, a story began to wrap itself around my heart. A story of life rising from the ashes of death; of hope shining brightly in the darkness; and of broken things being made new. It was a story that deeply touched me, and one I am honored to share.

Jodi Stuber, not only did I discover a story that needed to be told that morning at HopeWell, but I also found a dear friend. Thank you for trusting me with your story. And thank you for being such a source of encouragement, joy, and light in my life—as well as in the lives of so many. I'm really going to miss our weekly talks and countless texts. It has been a joy to work with you on this book.

To Ty, Amanda, Tania, and the rest of the HopeWell family, thank you for being so generous with your time and for being so supportive of this project.

A special thank-you to Jerry for sitting with me the night of the fall benefit and sharing your heart. Your words felt like a sacred gift—one I will never forget. Thank you for serving our country the way you did and for serving our veterans the way you do now. You are a true hero.

To Sarah Atkinson, Bonne Steffen, and the amazing team at Tyndale House, thank you for believing in this story and making it the book it is today. You all are such a gift to me and so many others. It is an absolute honor and joy to work with you.

Jessica Kirkland, I remember calling you from HopeWell after I met Jodi and telling you that I wanted to share her story. Thank you for catching the vision for this book and encouraging me to pursue it.

A big thank-you to Katie Reid for sitting in the dark parking lot with me after our joint book signing and letting me vision cast for this project. You provided a listening ear and wise counsel at a time I greatly needed both. I am so grateful for you.

Dave Schroeder, thanks for being such a great sounding board and for speaking into this project when I needed a second opinion.

A special thank-you to those who have been praying for me and this project, and who continually shine the hope and light of Jesus into my life:

Aimee and Julie, thank you for your prayers and for making sure I climbed out of my writing hole long enough to eat tacos with you!

Jodi Grubbs, thank you for sitting with me in various coffee shops around Raleigh and always being a safe place for me to process life, storylines, book ideas, and next steps.

Tracy and Carey, thank you for filling my phone with hilarious GIFs and always being just a text away.

Brooklyn Stephens, thank you for allowing me to wander around Arise Ranch and study your horses while I worked on this book. You are such a source of encouragement, support, and joy to our family.

Aunt Judy, thank you for continuing to be my biggest cheerleader and one of my dearest friends. Your support means so much.

Mom and Daddy, thank you for encouraging me to pursue this story and listening to me talk about these past several years. Your belief in me has always exceeded my own. I am so grateful to be your daughter and so thankful for you both.

To Darrell, Andrew, and Ella, you are my heart, my home, and my own treasured herd. Thank you for being my safe place and my favorite place. I love each one of you so very much.

I'd also like to offer a very special thank-you to our veterans and to those who are currently serving in the military. Thank you for your service and your sacrifice. I pray this book honors you and that you will always be able to glimpse a light of hope—even in the darkest night.

And finally, Father God, thank you for filling this earth with so many animals who help us, teach us, bring us such joy, and offer us glimpses of your own heart. This is all for you.

About the Authors

 **Jodi Stuber** is cofounder and executive director of HopeWell Ranch, a nonprofit therapy ranch founded in 2004 that provides free services for individuals, children, and families. HopeWell's programs include Unbridled Potential, a riding program for children with special needs, and Project Solomon, for veterans who are struggling with PTSD. Jodi and her husband, Ty, live in Weidman, Michigan, where they enjoy spending time with their children and grandchildren.

 **Jennifer Marshall Bleakley** is also the author of *Joey: How a Blind Rescue Horse Helped Others Learn to See*, as well as the Pawverbs devotional series. She has worked as a child and family grief counselor and holds a master's degree in mental health counseling from Nova Southeastern University. She lives in Raleigh, North Carolina, with her husband, Darrell, their two children, and a menagerie of animals. You can connect with Jen online at jenniferbleakley.com or on social media @jenbleakley.

Heart, Hooves, Healing . . . HOPE

HopeWell Ranch was founded in 2004 as a therapy farm with an emphasis on helping hurting children. This ministry has since evolved into assisting veterans, families, and individuals in their quest for healing. HopeWell Ranch partners with a variety of animals in a beautiful natural setting where people can connect to health in a peaceful farm atmosphere. Project Solomon, Unbridled Potential, Young Farmer and Friends, Project Aware, and Parenting from the Barn are some of the programs that the ranch currently provides to the community.

VISION STATEMENT
The love of Christ in action to encourage and empower struggling people to achieve hope, healing, and purpose.

MISSION STATEMENT
To create a loving environment of hope, healing, and purpose for children, individuals, and families, where lives can be transformed, in order to succeed, through the redeeming love of Christ.

HopeWell Ranch
6410 W. Leiter Rd.
Weidman MI 48893
989-644-5965

www.hopewellranch.org
info@hopewellranch.org
http://facebook.com/
HopeWellRanch
Instagram @hopewell_ranch

For I know the plans I have for you, says the LORD.
They are plans for good and not for disaster,
to give you a future and a hope.

JEREMIAH 29:11

Heartwarming tales of real-life pets, combined with inspiring truths about *love, devotion, and faith* from the book of Proverbs

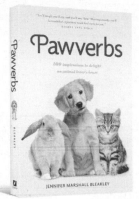